P9-DHO-990

# HOPE FOR YOUR TOMORROW

## *When Someone You Love Dies By Suicide...*

Grief Care
FELLOWSHIP

# FRANCIS WELCH

# Dedication

We dedicate this book to you, the survivor
of suicide.

Because someone special died by suicide, you have
been left confused and brokenhearted. You are living
through personal suffering and far-reaching
traumatic pain.

The dedication is not because you found all the
answers you searched for, nor because your heartache
has been resolved.

We want you to find courage in walking forward
with life, even when life itself feels as though it has no
purpose. This book is dedicated to you because
you will continue to live life.

The personal testimonies in this book are real-life
experiences of individuals who have walked where you
now walk, sharing their guidance of hope and faith.

Grief Care Fellowship®

# Table of Contents

# *Preface*

*M*y goal in sharing this book with you is specifically to provide help and encourage-ment to those that are known as "suicide survivors." You need to know that while you have experienced the death of your loved one by suicide, there is hope beyond your loss and pain.

For many years I experienced heartfelt empathy with those suffering the loss of a loved one. My ministry with those in pain was initially a one-on-one with friends and strangers. I learned to listen to grievers' heartache. But I knew that was not enough. I attended Bible college and received my degree in biblical studies and counseling.

After graduation, the Lord opened a ministry for me as a Minister of Care at Northcliffe Church of Spring Hill, FL. Through my local church ministry I found a ministry fitting my spiritual gift of mercy. As I reached out to hurting families, I kept hundreds of notes on what had proven effective in ministering to those in pain. Even more important, I kept notes and cards from individuals concerning their hope in their journey of grief.

This book, written for you as a suicide survivor, is the culmination of my ministering to others following all forms of death, including death by suicide. Over many years I have participated in numerous memorial services, including several deaths by suicide. Within these chapters you will find encouragement from those who walked this path before you and have left their wisdom and insights for your journey. Included also are several personal stories of individuals whose loved one died by suicide. Their life experiences will enable you to confront your questions and fears and to realize there is hope for tomorrow.

Grace and blessings,
Francis Welch

SEGMENT 1

# SEEKING HONEST ANSWERS

# CHAPTER 1

# *Introduction*

*M*y friend's vivid white hair flowed down across his forehead. On windy days it drifted from side to side, yet he made no attempt to keep it in place. His gestures portrayed an individual boisterous with laughter and he could keep me chuckling for extended periods of time. On the exterior he was an extroverted, caring, loving, giving individual. Within the depths of his inner spirit, however, he was painstakingly plagued by chaotic, emotional experiences.

For many years, during the Christmas season he loved playing Santa Claus. His overzealous temperament easily transformed him into the loving benefactor he portrayed. On occasion he slipped into a dark abyss. A seemingly desolate place I could not travel with him, nor would I ever choose to. For him, this darkness was a place where nothing was sensibly accomplished, where logic had no basis of understanding. Over the course of many years, he threatened suicide, attempted suicide, and one fateful night died by suicide. He was a good friend and even to this day I find myself often thinking of him. I will share more of his story later.

This book will not deal with the complicated layers of mental illnesses or provide any final answers to the insurmountable questions surrounding death by suicide. Multitudes of journalistic articles, psychological analyses, and therapeutic critiques have explored loss by suicide. Still, I considered including some formidable statistics on suicides–important data such as vocation, age, and culture, both within our country and worldwide. I even wondered about adding a section on suicide prevention and why your loved one may have failed to connect with a suicide hotline. Then I was reminded that all the statistics of suicide may mean nothing to you, the griever. The only statistic that matters is your loved one died by suicide. No chapter on suicide prevention could remove your devastation, answer your questions, or encourage your heart. Your loved one, unfortunately, already made that decision.

Instead, we will deal with death by suicide from an emotional health viewpoint. For many years suicide was considered a selfish, deliberate, and inexcusable form of death. Culture in general attached a stigma to this form of death. Therefore, the family and friends of someone who died by suicide were not expected to mourn as those who experienced traditional loss by death. Thankfully, today mental health issues are viewed from the same medical perspective as heart disease or cancer. Still, dying by suicide is a complicated issue. People living with a mental illness can experience unusual behaviors, which frequently are not of their own choosing. What is most important is for you to realize and accept that death by suicide, although traumatic, may very well not have been your loved one's rational choice.

Depression and additional mental illnesses are major risk factors for dying by suicide. Mental health advocates, to reduce the stigma of suicide, use the term "died by suicide." Some individuals choose to end their own lives due to a variety of factors: substance use disorder, clinical depression, financial hardships, debilitating pain, or terminal illness, a feeling of uselessness such as with older age, personal guilt over some issue, and numerous other reasons. We must realize that in most cases, individuals who lose their lives to death by suicide were incapable of preventing this death any more than those who die from heart problems or cancer.

Most deaths enable the griever to experience a healthy journey of grief, but other deaths, like suicide, can complicate that journey, as they seem more traumatic and tragic. Suicide is inclusive of men, women, young, old, rich, and poor. No one segment of society is immune to this type of tragedy. Deaths by suicide, unlike all other deaths, are unique. My experience has been that no two forms of death are ever the same. This is especially true in suicide. Every decision of death by suicide is distinctive. No matter how long and hard a griever may search for reasons, they may never find the complete answer to the "Why?" question.

For Christians, death by suicide leaves us with spiritual questions, not only concerning the suicide itself but also about how someone we love could choose to die in this manner. We seek to know not only why, but what does God say about it. We will share more on biblical issues in a forthcoming chapter.

CHAPTER 2

# *Difficulties of Acceptance*

*D*ealing with death by suicide may cause your inner spirit to feel like you have plunged into a bottomless cavern of no return. I remember one person sharing with me that she imagined herself hovering over a room, where the floor looked like a never-ending bottomless hole and that if she fell in, she could never come back. Her sheer desperation in dealing with tragic loss came from the fear that her pain would never end. Others have described this depth of pain as an unbearable devastation. They wish they could fall asleep, wake up, and find this all just a horrible nightmare. One individual in a grief group told me, "I was afraid to fall asleep for fear I would wake up and find his death to be true. I ultimately did find sleep and yes, I awoke to the reality of his death."

Facing your loved one passing away by suicide is an agonizing and overwhelming reality. You will have to deal with your awful pain and live with this legacy. You never would have anticipated that you would lose your loved one, it probably never crossed your mind. Every emotion within you does not or did not want to accept this truth. You may yell at your loved one, scream out your hurting emotions, and do something totally out of context for who you are. That is okay; you are no longer who you used to be. No words will ever describe the absolute loneliness of living life without your loved one. The roughest times are going to be when you expect your loved one to walk through the door, call or leave a message, hearing their voice or laughter. Missing your loved one's presence is the great heartache of loss. But as you confront your emotional agony, that confrontation itself will become a part of your healing process.

You may even find yourself angry with God. But it is imperative to believe the One who wants to help you most is God. He knows your pain better than anyone and He wants to give His comfort and strength to you. Through all your pain, hurt, questions, and devastation, He is beside you. He wants to hold you, support you, comfort you, and encourage you.

In times of crisis, we usually more intently open our hearts to seek God's grace and comfort. In all your aching heartache, He has never left you. God is right here, right now, within your heart. Psalm 100 reminds us that our Lord's steadfast love endures, and He is faithful. Yes, pain hurts, but far greater than our pain is the unwavering loving faithfulness of our Lord. So, we can live with our emotions bottled up or we can look to the encouragement, strength, and reassurance of our

Lord, the Great Comforter.

A wonderful reminder of the Lord's great comfort is found in the gospel of John, chapter 14. Jesus' disciples are greatly troubled and fearful. He instructs them that the Father will send His comforter (helper) who will be at their side forever. Do you grasp the truth of this promise? What a great assurance that in times of difficulties and trouble, we have the Holy Spirit, who is present at this very moment in your life. He dwells with you and in you.

CHAPTER 3

# "Why?" - "What If?" - "If Only"

Over numerous years I have read many books and publications on death by suicide. Yet despite my attempts to comprehend the "why" of suicide, the answers still elude me. Of all the issues surrounding the uncertainty of this tragedy, the single most often asked question I am asked is "Why?" Added to the shock and disbelief of death by suicide are the incredible personal guilt and the questions: "What could I have done?" "Why didn't I see the signs?" You as the griever are plagued by unbearable questions, unfortunately with no answers.

A professional counselor friend shared some thoughts with me on the "why" question:

> *The griever no longer has any opportunity to talk with their loved one, and even if the deceased left a note, many layers of unanswered questions remain. Suicide's "Why?" can become a haunting question. Any attempt to initially resolve it will only lead you to*

*explore many possible reasons, with no real answers. This form of immediate questioning can become more harmful than helpful. When you first learned of the suicide, your public and emotional expression was this question of why, in your need to understand what happened. "Why?" is your cry of pain. Later, perhaps months later, you will be able to have a more peaceful time to question and contemplate, and then be ready for some healthy discussion concerning death by suicide.*

I am confident that throughout your life you have experienced hundreds of "why" questions for many situations. But nothing compares to the profound questions surrounding suicide. As a griever of loss by suicide you naturally live with this huge unanswered question of "Why?" For weeks, even months, you will repeatedly ask yourself and others this question and endure the frustration of having no answer. The difficult answer to "Why?" is that only your loved one knows the ultimate reason behind their death by suicide. The reality is that you must leave the knowledge of this decision with him or her. Even if you had all the answers about your loss, you would still experience deep grief.

Most people who ultimately end their lives have

struggled, perhaps long and arduously, with issues they felt they were unable to resolve. Sometimes people experiencing severe depression determine that their families would be better off without them. The point is, no matter how many times you try to analyze the death; there is no stress-free answer. Ultimately your loved one's personal reasoning led to the decision. You must accept the fact that you may never know why.

Try to understand that even though your loved one left behind many unanswered questions, your emotions of heartache, sorrow, disillusionment, and perhaps anger or bitterness complicate your grieving process. The tough truth is that your loved one probably never considered the deep pain you would experience. It probably was not their intent to inflict such anguish upon your soul. With a lack of rationality, their thinking was probably so blurred and overwhelmed they had no connection to reality. Your loved one most likely thought they were making the best possible decision given their emotional state at that time.

Your loved one did not have an accurate connection to the devastation their action would leave behind. I imagine most of the time the one contemplating suicide feels as though they are not only making a rational decision but also the best possible choice for themselves and others. You know they did not; I know they did not. Yet you are left to pick up the pieces and deal with the pain. You are left with the pain of asking "Why?" and having no answer.

You also may wonder how you missed the warning signs. And you deal with the awful guilt that you should have done more, tried something else, or at the very least prevented the suicide. You search your mind, wondering and seeking answers. You brood over whether you could have been a better or more loving spouse, mom, dad, grandparent, sibling, or friend. But most of all you agonize over "Why?" Your heart is burdened with the questions of why you did not see any signs of the pending suicide in your loved one's words or behavior. Your heart and emotions toss and turn with the questions: Why did I not see this? How could I have missed the warning signs? And inevitably, was this my responsibility?

I remember one parent sharing with me, "It has to be somebody's fault; she would not have done this on her own." Please believe me. It was not your fault. Sometimes those we have a deep and abiding love for make decisions that are irrational. Dying by suicide is one of them. Yes, you believe if they had shared their desperate thoughts with you, at least you could have provided some form of intervention. Unfortunately, most suicides are thought about and planned in secret, without professional intervention. One of the most challenging problems is that, unfortunately, even with intervention and mediation, a suicidal person still makes that permanent choice, and you are not responsible for that choice.

CHAPTER 4

# God's Overwhelming Grace
## *Joy's Story*

G od has led me through three traumatic events of life—the death by suicide of both of my husbands and my brother. As a young mother, I enjoyed life with my pastor husband as we ministered to the youth of our community. How could I have known or expected that the love of my life would die by suicide? Several years later God blessed me with a second husband who would also traumatically die by suicide. The immense depths of my pain left me with deep agony and heartache that you are also experiencing.

As I share my journey of profound loss with you, I want you to know I have walked where you now walk. My purpose now is to tell you that our loving heavenly Father has promised His comfort and love. He will never leave you. He is present in this journey with you. I know because I have experienced His faithful love and grace. May you find trust in God and His promises of faith, hope, and the same peace He has given me.

*My First Husband, Ken*

Ken and I enjoyed a fun, loving marriage for seven years. We had a four-and-a-half-year-old daughter and I was nine months pregnant with our second child when Ken died. He was a youth minister, living such a godly life, professionally and personally. A difficult pastoral church issue came up that greatly affected Ken's emotional health. He never had any previous history of depression and no history of mental health issues in his family. He sought professional counseling, followed all the counselor's guidance, and took prescribed medications. The day of his death, as I waited for the ambulance to arrive, I recall thinking to myself that I did everything I could have done for Ken. I even asked him once if he was considering suicide and he told me no, that he loved our daughter and me too much.

I was expecting the arrival of our second child at any time. And before that day, to me, Ken was doing so much better. Our life was moving forward. As Ken's mental health improved, his psychiatrist began to wean him off his medications, and I was excited for him. Then suddenly, unbeknownst to any of us and without any warning, Ken's mental health abruptly declined. On that Monday, the most unexpected and traumatic event in my life occurred. Ken died by suicide. On Wednesday of the same week, we held a memorial service for Ken, and on Friday I gave birth to our son. My son never got to see his dad, and Ken never got to know his son.

Ken's death was traumatic for me. Now my future was being a mom with two wonderful children but living life without a loving husband. I found myself devastated and alone. I felt like a complete train wreck without Ken. I hated the evenings especially when it was time to close the blinds. I felt that every other family was all back together for the night, but ours was just the three of us with Ken very much missing from our home.

I felt so hurt by God. I felt like God placed me on a stage in front of everyone and just slapped me in my face. I was in such shock. I sincerely believed we had been living our family life just as God wanted us to, faithfully serving Him in the church ministry He had called us to. This horrific pain in my relationship with God lasted a long time.

### Support from Ken's Family and My Church

After Ken's death, my life seemed like a blur, and for three years I struggled with the pain of loss. Ken's parents were so supportive of me and my two children. Even in the depths of their own pain, they were right with me in planning Ken's memorial service. I could not think what to do or how to do it, but his parents were right beside me. In my depths of despair, I could not even decide where to bury my husband. We had a cremation and memorial service, but it would be six months before I could decide about his final resting place.

My church family was an amazing group of encouragers. They joined together to do the practical things that had to be done. Some walked alongside me with encouragement and strength. Being overwhelmed with grief and trying to meet the needs of my new baby left me emotionally and physically exhausted. My church small group designed a unique chart, and every couple of nights someone would come to help with needs–such as laundry and folding clothes–and to stay overnight. My friends at church pulled together as a compassionate group, consistently, in critical and unique ways to care for me and my children. The care, love, and encouragement from my home church was so special.

*My Healing*

I experienced many months where I just wanted to go out into the nearby woods and scream. I needed a release for all the pain, confusion, and hurt. I was obsessed with figuring out how God could let this happen to my husband. I began to learn about the grieving journey God sets before us after loss. At an early point, I was surprised how my friend's and family's lives seemed to go on as usual. I learned this was an expected part of the grieving process, so I began to understand this and tried to accept it.

Early on after Ken's death, many of my friends recommended I see a counselor, but I brushed them off. I literally remember thinking after one friend suggested it again, *"OK, I'll go to the counselor to just be able to say I went"*. This was a life-changer for me. I saw the benefit of seeing him each week, at first to unload everything I was going through, and he helped me find healthy ways to move through my grief. I believe counseling is an important part of a person's grief journey.

As I walked this journey of grief, I realized I needed to have some specific goals. One of my goals was to reach a point where even though I was alone, I would not feel lonely. This took me two and a half years, but it was rewarding to get to that place of strength in my life.

### My Second Husband, Jimmy

Jimmy's death by suicide also caught me by complete surprise. I was filled with disbelief that such a loss could happen to me again. Experiencing the entire roller coaster of emotions, my questions centered on how I did not see Jimmy's death coming. The emotions of what I should have or could have done differently filled my mind constantly. As I grieved the loss of my second husband, Jimmy, I again faced the challenge to learn how to be alone, yet not lonely. While I am much older this time, the loss of my second husband has brought extreme loneliness in my grief.

Grieving Jimmy's death has been every bit as hard as grieving Ken's. Even though I am much older now than when Ken died, and a much more mature Christian, I am moving through the entire painful grief process as I had to move through it with Ken thirty years earlier. Two important realizations have helped me. The first is that I was long ago acquainted with the grief process, which helped me have some expectations of what might come next as I mourned Jimmy's death. In a sense it helped in a small way to buffer the pain.

The second insight is that with my first husband, I wholly experienced God's plan of grief that He designed when we lose someone we love. I fully grieved Ken and was able to reach the point where I could live with the terrible loss of him, but not have to face the terrible pain of that loss every day. I now focus on that during this time of grief for Jimmy, fully believing that once again, as I move forward in grief, I will always feel the loss but will not always have to feel this pain.

God has been so faithful to allow me wisdom in dealing with not only my pain but the many things I had to handle. He reminded me I was not to camp in my pain nor live in the past but have faith that He will bring me to a point of living a productive life once again, filled with meaning and joy.

## Moving Forward

One of the most important purposes in all my sorrow, heartache, and pain is the realization that God was preparing me for a greater ministry. And that is also true for you. We can stay where we are, we can live in regret, or we can allow God to minister through us and prepare us to minister to other hurting individuals. The Bible reminds us that God has comforted us so that we in turn can be a comfort to others (2 Corinthians 1:3-4). God has allowed me to minister to others who are walking the journey I once walked. We all tend to think that tomorrow will be the same as today, but when the death of a loved one occurs, everything changes.

Grief is a long and demanding journey, but our Lord walks beside you. Sometimes friends can be awkward with what or how they share with you, but God always knows what you need. He will honor your faith, trust, and hope. I have been blessed to honor the memory of both my husbands by helping you and others walk through their pain.

It is so important for you to move forward with living life, even if it is a step at a time. That is what the grief journey is, moving on with life, as difficult and emotionally exhausting as it is. Life does go on. You will never forget your loss, but you will learn to live with it. Yes, your journey to healing will sometimes be slow going, on occasion going backward, but learn to keep trusting God. Trust Him to keep you safe and secure in His grace. I can look back now and assure you that my grief was raw, and at times I hit rock bottom. I did not have to stay there and neither do you. We make choices to move forward. We either make life better or we become bitter. The choice was mine and now it is yours.

CHAPTER 5

# *Choose What to Remember*

A s Minister of Care, I instinctively knew visiting this family would be exceedingly difficult. I knew they were enduring the deepest pains of grief, still reeling from the recent suicide of a family member. Affectionately known as Artie, he had been a husband, father, and grandfather, but all that had recently changed with his tragic death, determined to be death by suicide. Two weeks earlier, this family was planning a vacation. Now they barely existed. Instead of a vacation, they had to plan a funeral. Instead of taking memorable new family photos, they searched former photos for a memorial service. And instead of enjoying fun family times, they were mired down in demanding emotional pain.

During my visit with them, I was not prepared for the volatility of passions shared by the family. One family member thought it helpful to share about his father, recounting his enjoyment of life, love of family, faithfulness at church, and employment. He shared about the positive legacy his dad had left behind.

Another family member's conversation quickly turned to the difficult hurt and pain Dad had caused. As one of the sons wept over his dad's death, he mourned that the father had left behind a horrible legacy of death by suicide.

Almost every family member lamented that Artie would not be remembered as a loving father and husband but rather as "the one who died by suicide." Mom bitterly thought that in the future, when she remembered her husband, it would not be in love, but anger and bitterness for how he chose to end his life. I realized that much of this hurtful thinking was based on the family's deep emotional pain. Yet I also knew they had to release their anger, frustrations, and endless "Why?" questions. All their hurt and pain had to be dealt with, and it would take many months to assist them in walking through their mourning and loss. For one family member, professional therapy with a Christian counselor was supportive and helpful in her journey through deep grief.

Even with your heartache and roller coaster emotions, it is critical for you to remember and enjoy fond memories and share family stories of better times. As real and tough as this time will be, you do have the promise that one day, depending upon your journey of faith; you will be reunited in heaven again. Despite your grief, seek to grasp and understand that your loved one's legacy does not need to be buried or hidden away. It is okay and healthy to share those fond memories, the good times, their talents, and strengths, and how they lived life. Your loved one's life was important—it mattered, and their presence and time with you did have meaning and purpose. Perhaps the greatest promise I can leave with you is that you will make it through this journey. You will heal and live life again.

CHAPTER 6

# Immediate Disbelief

You are experiencing the disbelief that your loved one died by suicide. You are asking overwhelming questions with few, if any, answers. I can never forget the griever who sorrowfully shared their family's story. For several years, the family anticipated the suicide of their loved one but did nothing to intervene. They feared confronting their loved one because they valued the relationship and knew confrontation meant rejection. After the loss of this loved one, the family could not resolve personal conflicts and believed they were at fault for not somehow preventing the death. Even though they anticipated the suicide, they still experienced profound disbelief and frustration at its actual occurrence.

Many grievers experience shocking, personal disbelief when a loved one dies by suicide. Not one of us ever expects our loved one to make this choice. I recall one suicide survivor, who shared that her dad on occasion talked about dying by suicide. She felt his interest was only a subject he wanted to try to understand. She did not realize his inquiries were his way of reaching out for help nor that he was contemplating his own death.

Another suicide survivor related that she never expected the suicide and recalled no actions that would have led her to even consider suicide was in her sister's mind. She was in absolute astonishment. In her disbelief she denied the truth. The sudden shockwave left her emotionally unable to cope. Unable to grasp the facts, she refused to believe such extreme news. In the immediacy of finding out, she wanted to close her eyes and ears—*"If I can't see or hear, then it is not true."* Life for her became like living in a fog where she did not and could not face reality. Finally, after a couple of weeks, reality set in, the haze lifted, and she began to deal with the harshness of loss by suicide's reality.

How intensely you probably recall those first few moments, hours, and days of confusion, disbelief, and misunderstanding. You may have felt you were living outside of yourself and just going through the motions of life. In the immediate weeks and months, you will be reminded of every painful emotion you experienced that day. It is as though you will feel yourself frozen in time. You may presently be in a time and place where even though it is impossible to reconcile the suicide, you have accepted the harsh reality of it.

Suicide is often the result of numerous

mental health issues. It is not a character flaw or lack of personal discipline. This final choice by a loved one can be based on multiple levels of difficult circumstances or the wearisome of living life. Maybe it was a culmination of trying to cope with life, which seemed to offer no alternatives and no end to the current hopeless situation. All the "bottled up" emotions came together, intermingling like a short-circuited electrical impulse. Your loved one lost their capacity to survive in those final moments or hours. For reasons we do not comprehend, they lost all hope, saw no future, and had no answers, and ultimately envisioned no future.

Former grievers shared some typical comments such as:

- *"He hid his true feelings and intent."*

- *"She did not discuss suicide with me."*

- *"He seemed so much better than usual."*

- *"If only I had known, I could have stopped him."*

- *"Why was I so naive not to believe them when they spoke of suicide?"*

Despite our thoughts and disbelief, we must deal with reality, which can be tough. We want to go back and change what happened. But no matter how intently we want to be able to change something—

anything—about that fateful day, we cannot. The inflexible truth cannot be changed. At some point the pieces of life must be picked up and we must move forward with living life. Guilt, the "if only," and "wish I had" keep us in the past, preventing us from dealing with our present pain or moving forward. Some of the saddest words I hear are "If only I had..."

Grief is one of the most difficult passages of life to walk alone. There will be those who will listen, care, comfort, and encourage. But you will find you will walk your own path. Your suffering heart, denials, anger, and personal loss can seem overwhelming. Seek God's healing, focusing on His hope, grace, and peace. He will sustain you.

# CHAPTER 7

# *Hope Beyond Today*

*H*ope is one of the paramount assurances throughout scripture. The author of Hebrews writes, "We have this hope as an anchor for the soul, firm and secure" (Hebrews 6:19). Hope is a central biblical promise we as believers have, but those without faith cannot experience. From the world's perspective, hope is an optimistic state of feeling. To nonbelievers, hope is an expectation of an affirmative outcome of events and circumstances within the structure of their lives. In other words, for those outside of spiritual faith, hope is merely an anticipation of "whatever will be, will be" or "I hope it will be better." The world's system offers hope, but it is make-believe, and false hope is no hope. Without a biblical foundation, hope becomes a wishy-washy expectation.

For the Christian, hope has a far-reaching and greater depth than just a simple "I hope so." Biblical hope is the active application of our faith that results in confident expectation that God fulfills His promises.

1 Corinthians 13 combines hope with faith and love; they are connected. Hope is a basic building block of the Christian life. Hope in scripture reflects a resilient, assured expectation—a confidence in the future that we yet do not comprehend or understand. Your hope is your foundational faith in trusting God and is based on knowledge of His love for you. He can complete that which is above and beyond what you may ever think, feel, or imagine. Allow yourself to patiently walk with God as He infuses grace, peace, and encouragement into your broken heart. You may not "see" the hope, but it is there, and God will permeate His hope into your life.

> *"For in this hope, we were saved. But hope that is seen is no hope at all. Who hopes for what they already have? But if we hope for what we do not yet have, we wait for it patiently."*
>
> (Romans 8:24-25)

We do not visually see hope; it is a spiritual blessing—as are the inner spiritual truths of God's love, grace, and peace—through the Holy Spirit. We do not "see" them, but they are nevertheless genuine. We believe all of this to be a reality. Hope is our confident expectation, complete trust, and assurance of an active and dynamic relationship that God promised us in His word, one that is and will be reality.

Hope plays an integral part of our journey

through grief. First, it causes us to have assurance that if our loved one knew the Lord, we will meet them again in heaven. We are reminded in 1 Thessalonians 4:13 that we do not grieve as those who have no hope. We have the promised confidence of seeing loved ones again. Second, we realize that this life is but a vapor (James 4:13-17) and we also shall one day be present in heaven. Life is incredibly short, but those in the Lord continue to live on in glory. Third, hope changes what we value in this life. As we look to the future, we realize we are but sojourners passing through this world. Our hope is not on the material but on the spiritual. As we reflect on the death of our loved one, the former material things of life seem to fade away. Hebrews 11:13 reminds us we are just aliens and strangers on this earth. Fourth, scripture gives us many promises rooted in hope, joy and peace (Romans 15:13); in times of calamity, we are under God's loving care (Psalm 33:18) strength and courage (Psalm 31:24); concerning heaven, we have comfort and confidence (1 Thessalonians 4:13); and we have assurance in this life to continue serving our Lord (1 Timothy 4:10).

Our hope arises from the powerful love of God, and hope is His way of ministering to you. You are not alone. He knows your frailty in asking questions. He hears your heart. He has a continuing plan for your life. "For I know the plans I have for you," declares the LORD, "plans to prosper you and not to harm you, plans to give you hope and a future" (Jeremiah 29:11). Hope is God's manner of reaching down to you. Are you reaching out to Him?

As grievers, walking this journey, the Lord identifies with your pain. He is here to comfort you. Your loved one's suicide did not catch God by surprise. Maybe it surprised you, but not God. We must cling to truths of Scripture that our Lord loves us and intimately desires to minister to us. You will find great comfort that your loved one is securely in His presence.

# CHAPTER 8

# *Biblical Perspective of Suicide*

*A*s a minister, I value the biblical view of suicide. Some grievers ask such questions as "What does the Bible say about suicide?" and "Are people who die by suicide eternally separated from God?" In scripture God promises His forgiving grace, a grace inclusive of those who have died by suicide. Still, this question persists: "Can a believer, who has been forgiven of sins and welcomed into the family of God through God's grace and mercy, do something that becomes unforgiveable? Can we somehow lose our spiritual identity, our standing in Christ, or the witness of the Spirit that we are the children of God?" (See Romans 8:14-17.)

I am convinced of the eternal security of the Christian in Jesus Christ. If our loved one knew the Lord, that is the only basis of assurance of heaven. Our righteousness and standing before God are not based on how we performed, or our acts of obedience, but on the ultimate submission of Jesus at Calvary.

Your loved one made a decision we can never

understand, but I am convinced from biblical truth that death by suicide for the Christian does not result in eternal separation from God. For the one who is a "child of God," nothing will ever separate them from Him.

A Christian counselor shared these thoughts with me:

> *"Some faiths teach that suicide is an unpardonable sin and therefore the one who died by suicide is not promised eternal life in heaven. The only biblical unpardonable sin is refusing God's offer of forgiveness in Christ. Biblically, there is forgiveness of all sin, including the taking of one's own life. This is important because the suicide survivor is left with a deep fear of where their loved one is spending eternity."*

Scripture contains many references to the security of the believer. The apostle Paul, in Romans, chapter 8, shares that we as believers are free of condemnation and that God resides in us (Romans 8:1, 9). Romans 8:39 says, "Nor anything else in all of creation, will be able to separate us from the love of God that is in Christ Jesus our Lord."

The following are encouraging scriptures regarding the assurance of being in God's presence when we have received Christ:

- We have the promise of eternal life:
  - *"For God so loved the world that he gave his only begotten Son, that whosoever believeth in him should not perish, but have everlasting life"* (John 3:16, KJV).

  - *"And this is the will of him who sent me that I shall lose none of all those he has given me but raise them up at the last day"* (John 6:39).

- Salvation is by grace; works cannot affect it:
  - *"For I am convinced that neither death nor life, neither angels nor demons, neither the present nor the future, nor any powers, neither height nor depth, nor anything else in all creation, will be able to separate us from the love of God that is in Christ Jesus our Lord"* (Romans 8:38-39).

- Nothing can separate believers from the love of Christ:
  - *"My sheep listen to my voice; I know them, and they follow me. I give them eternal life, and they shall never perish; no one will snatch them out*

*of my hand. My Father, who has given them to me, is greater than all; no one can snatch them out of my Father's hand"* (John 10:27-29).

- We are kept secure by the power of God:
  - *"Who through faith are shielded by God's power until the coming of the salvation that is ready to be revealed in the last time"* (1 Peter 1:5).

- We have been preserved unto the heavenly kingdom:
  - *"The Lord will rescue me from every evil deed and bring me safely into His heavenly kingdom. To Him is the glory forever and ever. Amen"* (2 Timothy 4:18, ESV).

- Ultimately believers will appear with Christ in glory:
  - *"When Christ, who is your life, appears, then you also will appear with him in glory"* (Colossians 3:4).

I realize some would say that any person who knows and loves Jesus, having experienced saving grace, could never purposely die by suicide. While it is tough to comprehend, the reality is that yes, it does happen. When we look at the lives of Christians throughout history, we know they endured and even suffered through incomprehensible personal times of depression. I have never experienced depression so I cannot grasp a mental health issue. I have never walked those journeys, never felt that emotional pain, but I have family and friends who have. And I do know that God's grace is ever present. We may never understand our loved one's suicide, but our sovereign God does.

I recognize as a minister that in this area of deep pain, I must leave my personal heart-wrenching questions with the Lord. Sometimes Christians, unfortunately and tragically, during hopelessness, lose sight of the glorious truth of life in Christ. The greatest encouragement I can give you is that our Lord, who is "rich in mercy" and loves us with a great love, has assured us of a heavenly promise." (See Ephesians 2:4-10.) Your loved one, as a believer, is securely at peace with the Lord.

The Bible mentions six specific individuals who died by suicide:

1. Samson was a great man of God, yet he allowed his personal passions to rule over his desire to serve his God. The final episode of his life finds him shackled to two columns of the temple, mocked, and scorned by the enemies of God. And Samson said, "Let me die with the Philistines." Then he bowed with all his

strength and the house fell upon all the people who were in it." In his great drive for revenge, Samson was willing to die when he killed the Philistines in the crowded temple that day. Braced between two pillars, he used his final strength to wrench them down and take his own life, along with his enemies. (See Judges 16:25-30, ESV.)

2. A great battle had ensued, and King Saul, along with his forces, lost the battle. Saul was seriously wounded. Because he did not want the enemy to kill him, he requested his armor-bearer to end his life. The armor-bearer refused, and Saul decided to fall on his own sword. (See 1 Samuel 31:3-5.)

3. When Saul's armor-bearer saw that Saul was dead, he fell likewise upon his sword and died. (See 1 Samuel 31:5.)

4. Ahithophel, a one-time close companion of David, and grandfather of Bathsheba, eventually took up the cause of Absalom's rise against King David. He realized his advice had not been taken and led to defeat over David's army. He then, in great discouragement, fear, rejection, and desperation, chose to go home. "He set his house in order and hanged himself" (See 2 Samuel 17:23, ESV).

5. Zimri, after defeat in battle, sensing utter personal defeat, saw no way out of his personal predicament except to end his own life. "And when Zimri saw that the city was taken, he went into the citadel of the king's house and burned the king's house over him with fire and died" (See 1 Kings 16:18, ESV).

6. Judas, in great despair and burden of guilt after betraying Christ, chose to die by suicide. This section of scripture is probably the most well-known description in the Bible on the tragedy of this form of death. Judas knew the Lord, walked, and ministered with Him. Yet he betrayed Jesus. In tremendous guilt and unable to reconcile his treachery, his own personal decision was suicide. He allowed his great weight of sin to lead him to this dreadful end. "And throwing down the thirty pieces of silver into the temple, he departed, and he went and hanged himself" (See Matthew 27:3-4, ESV).

These biblical accounts help us realize that suicide is inclusive in scripture. God chose, for better or worse, to record these events. God elected not to hide suicide from His Word to us. Death by suicide happens within our families, our circle of friends, and the church. Why should the church hide this painful truth? Suicide deaths within the Christian community can be difficult for most to comprehend. It confuses us because we want to believe a person of faith can find a better way out of despair. We ask why the person did not seek help from other believers, counselors, or the scriptures. One reality is that just as with any decision in the Christian life, individuals have the freedom to make their own decisions, for better or worse.

Those considering suicide tend to take all the encouragements and rejections, deliberate them against their feelings, and make their decision. Counselors share that the people considering suicide just do not see any way out of their dilemma. They see no positive option to choose. We must remember that those who choose suicide may be besieged with negative issues far beyond our comprehension. Your loved one battled their emotional issue with seemingly no solution, and perhaps even suffered a mental illness. These combinations can prove devastating.

CHAPTER 9

# Is Suicide the Unpardonable Sin?
## Dr. Marshall Wicks

*I* want to share with you about one of the unfortunate stigmas that often complicates the healing process after the suicide of a loved one. The social and emotional effects of suicide are traumatic enough without having to deal with additional stress created by the theological confusion that has attached itself to the issue. This confusion, and that is what it is, is centered around the misunderstanding of two passages: 1 John 1:9, which says that if we confess our sins, He is faithful and just to forgive our sins, and Matthew 12:31-32: "Therefore I say to you, every sin and blasphemy shall be forgiven people, but blasphemy against the Spirit will not be forgiven. And whoever speaks a word against the Son of Man will be forgiven, but whoever speaks against the Holy Spirit will not be forgiven, either in this age or in the age to come" (ESV). This second passage is also found in Mark 3:28-29.

There are many subtle variations in how these verses are used, but the general idea goes something like this: since any sin that we confess will be forgiven, then the unpardonable sin must be a sin that we cannot confess. Suicide is touted as the only guaranteed unconfessable sin and therefore must be the unpardonable sin.

This teaching is wrong on both counts. First, given how it handles 1 John, we would be culpable if we failed to confess a sin and died unexpectedly. We would live in constant fear. The word translated *confess* literally means "to say the same." It is a faith word for a works world. Trusting God involves agreeing with God. We can all agree with God that sin is bad, but can we stop sinning? I think not. John tells us in 1 John 1:8 that if we say that we do not sin, we deceive ourselves and the truth is not in us. So if we refuse to "say the same" as God about our sin, we raise a question about our faith not necessarily or directly about our salvation. Remember what John says in 1 John 5:4: faith is the victory that overcomes the world. People who trust God do sin, but they look for faith solutions not works solutions. The Pharisees who Jesus was talking to in Matthew wanted works solutions to faith problems. Faith people accept righteousness; they do not earn it.

That leads us to the second problem with the idea that suicide is the unpardonable sin: the context in Matthew and Mark. As Jesus talks with the Pharisees in both Matthew and Luke, He is addressing the true nature of righteousness. Where does our righteousness come from? Does "not sinning" make a person righteous? The Pharisees thought so. Jesus tells them that true righteousness can only be given as a gift by God. It cannot be earned. Righteous behavior can only be provided by the Holy Spirit. If we try to do the "righteousness thing" without the Holy Spirit, we are doomed to fail in this life and the next. There is no salvation apart from the work of the Spirit in our lives. Can such people commit sins like suicide? Of course, they can! Note what James 2:9 says: "If you obey every law except one, you are still guilty of breaking them all" (CEV).

I think it is safe to conclude that we should not put suicide in a separate category from other sins. In fact, we must continue to believe that salvation is an open door for any that hunger and thirst after righteousness, and that like all the gifts of God it is irrevocable.

Dr. Marshall Wicks
Professor
Word of Life Bible Institute

# SEGMENT 2

# PERSONAL ANXIETY

CHAPTER 10

# *Your Silent Walk*

*I* often think of the journey in grief as a silent walk because it is a journey only you, the griever, can process. Grievers whose loved ones experienced this form of death face an across-the-board solitary journey. Your life is filled with unanswerable questions that create enormous emotional and physical duress. Your silent walk is filled to overflowing with issues only you can resolve. It is represented by long arduous nights of seeking answers where there are none.

Compounding your grief, others ask you questions, and you realize they also have no answers. I recall one mom who shared that after the suicide of her daughter, a friend asked, "What happened?" Her immediate inner response was *"How do I know what happened, I am in a state of shock and disbelief; and you ask me what happened?"*

Another griever shared:

> *"When asked, I just turned and walked away. I had no answer to give. I was living a life with no responses; my*

*innermost world had become private. I could feel the staggering depth of pain but could not share that pain. It was mine and mine alone. Over the ensuing weeks I was asked time and time again the question "What happened?" and my mind could not formulate an answer."*

Another shared:

*"I remember one day going to the bank to retrieve personal papers from my safe deposit box and thinking to myself how much my hurt emotions are also locked away in a vault. I knew they were there, but I could not retrieve them. On some days it felt good knowing my emotions were locked away; other days I just wanted to scream, releasing those emotions so everyone could see them. I learned over time to keep my harshest emotions locked away from others. Some people did not understand, some did not want to listen, and some did not care. Ultimately, I began to understand that while my feelings were locked away in my vault, God knew the combination. He used my quiet times, scripture readings, and loving and caring friends to allow my inner spirit to heal."*

*Disenfranchised griever* is a term counselor's use that is associated with grievers who feel left out of the normal grieving process. When someone experiences loss by suicide, others, even close friends, sometimes do not know what to say or do, or how to react. They want to do, say, or share something but do not know what or how. Even sending a sympathy card can seem out of place. Therefore, these friends say and do nothing. As the griever, you can feel like no one wants to be around you. At the very least you may think no one cares.

I have learned over the years that when I am with a family feeling disenfranchised, the best approach I can take is to just sit and listen. I do not have the answers to "Why?" so why pretend to offer such answers? The best ministry I can have is simply being there, sharing scriptural thoughts of comfort.

One other term used with grievers is *ministry of presence*. Often the person grieving desires someone to just come alongside and listen to the silence. The ministry of presence is just that, coming alongside you and being a friend, offering no answers, platitudes, or clichés. How fortunate you are to have such a person as a friend. They seem to know, feel, or understand your hurt and are willing to just sit and listen to you, and say nothing at all. Sometimes silence is a great comforter.

CHAPTER 11

# Whispers

*I*n my ministry I have known of several suicides. Some were folks I never met, some I knew casually, and on one occasion I experienced the suicide of a close friend. In every instance I have heard the "whispers" surrounding suicide, the reluctance to use the word, and even the refusal to accept the suicide. I choose the word *whispers* because, unfortunate as it is, when we do not know the cause of something, in this case, suicide, we are careful not to articulate the cause of death. Instead, we whisper about it, as though death by suicide is a shameful decision, an inappropriate, self-purposeful choice.

This form of death is not based on wise discernment, truth, or emotional stability. Yet mental illness is a personal, complicated journey, and I do not profess to have professional training to comprehend or understand how it may impact death by suicide.

Once I received a call from a friend whose neighbor had recently died, requesting I visit the family. When I arrived at the home, I was informed the person had died the previous day and no one in the family was in a responsive mood. I asked one of the neighbors what happened. He recounted to me a lengthy story of how the man was cleaning his gun and it accidentally discharged and killed him. He then shared with me that some people thought it was suicide, but he knew better because his neighbor was a "great guy to be around." He additionally shared with me that his neighbor would not have committed suicide because he was "not that stupid" and that suicide was for "losers." Shortly after this conversation, I finally spoke to the family and when I asked the cause of death, one family member immediately and angrily told me, "It was not suicide, no matter what the police or coroner might say." Then in an emotional outburst, one family member told me their church would not do the funeral if the cause of death was determined as suicide. Part of their church doctrine was that suicide is the "unpardonable sin," and therefore the church would not conduct the deceased loved one's funeral.

In all the raw emotions of that moment, I did not take time to explain the truth about the biblical "unpardonable sin"; rather, I chose to console the family in their loss and offer to lead the memorial service. The family asked only one thing of me at the funeral, and that was not to use the word *suicide*. For the family, the word had been only whispered as a stigma surrounding the cause of death. Eventually they moved to another state, taking with them the hidden truth of their loved one's death.

This unfortunate illustration of death by suicide is seen in how both family and neighbor's perception of suicide was based on incorrect assumptions. Each person assumed the individual who died decided to die by suicide based on his own sinful volition. They failed to understand the impact of a mental illness on such a choice.

CHAPTER 12

# *Blame Game*

*B*laming others is an easy alternative to dealing with your pain. Blaming yourself is an even worse alternative. Tough as it may seem, suicide often is the result of a mental illness. Why are we so fearful to accept that our loved one just was not rational when they chose death by suicide? Their emotional process may have included self-questions such as "Should I, or shouldn't I?" "Will I, or won't I?" In the final analysis an emotional, irrational thought process influenced how they would end their life.

Difficult as it is to understand, your loved one made the decision to answer their own questions of "how, when, and where." You know the final answer they chose, but it does not mean you understand. The horrific truth is that you probably never expected your loved one to die by suicide. The horrendous weight of trying to comprehend their final choice can be emotionally crushing. One loved one shared, "I struggle with wanting to know the answers for his suicide, but the truth is I will never understand this tragedy, I will never understand his state of mind, and I will never find a satisfactory explanation."

Maybe your loved one left you a personal note. I remember one griever sharing with me: "I wish he had not left a note. It only hurts me so much more for him to write that he loved me, and I would understand. No, I do not understand at all."

Eventually you will have to live with unanswered questions. You must learn to gradually let go of the why questions and accept that your loved one took with them both the secretive areas of their life and the mystery of their death. Acceptance is crucial for you to move forward and continue to go on living life.

Your journey of grief can become incredibly complex. Even when you accept the fact that the death was not your fault, you will still deal with layers of emotions. Anger and bitterness may smolder beneath the surface of what others view as your "acceptable" grief process. Grief becomes complicated when you take on the emotions of fear, shame, and guilt. When we cannot figure out why something happened, we tend to place blame somewhere. You may not feel as if you are to blame, then it must be your loved one, a medical team, a health care provider, your church, a friend, or some agency. After all, they all should have recognized and prevented the death.

The one truth you can grasp onto is that you will make it, you will survive, and you will live life again. God will heal your heart. Jesus, sharing with His disciples, instructed them, "Do not let your hearts be troubled" (John 14:1, NIV). It will take time, but God's grace, peace, and love will heal your broken heart, and you will be able to let go of the blame you have assigned to others or yourself.

## CHAPTER 13

# *Stigma*

*U*nfortunately, stigma is still a major issue when it comes to death by suicide. I am finding, however, that within the Christian community it has slowly become more acceptable to discuss this issue. We now live in a more transparent and honest society that recognizes loss through suicide as a necessary cultural awareness. When it comes to discussing suicide prevention and bereavement counseling of suicide, this new openness is a welcome and healthy change.

My pastor, when presiding at memorial services of loss by suicide, always shares the love and grace of God. But he also shares that the deceased had not made a rational choice in ending their life. He felt it was crucial for individuals to understand that death by suicide does not separate the deceased from their Lord, and that dying by suicide is not an unpardonable sin. But he also knew that both the family and others in attendance needed to realize suicide is not an answer to life's problems.

If the death cannot be talked about openly, the journey of grief will not be healthy and not healing. Still, some family members or friends may attach a stigma to suicide, and this unfortunately will lead to avoidance, leaving you to suffer alone in silence. Stigma is the labeling and misunderstanding of mental disorders in general and of suicide. Unfortunately, even with mental illness and suicide education and awareness, some people incorrectly conclude that mental issues are the result of family dysfunctions, personal weaknesses, or some character flaw. The reality is that a mental illness typically develops much like any genetic illness such as heart disease, cancer, diabetes, and other forms of illness. Unfortunately, this is not always recognized. The death of a person with a mental illness who dies by suicide is not accepted by family or friends in the same grieving patterns as other types of death. Many people find it difficult to talk about suicide and so they deliberately avoid using the term.

Once, as I listened to a griever whose son had committed suicide, she related how "Everyone must see this as a personal family failure." Nothing is further from the truth.

You probably have struggled with what to tell others. You may experience a sense of shame because of the way your loved one died. You want to protect your loved one's character from any type of diminished memories.

There are three important truths for you to recognize concerning stigmas:

- First, it is emotionally healthy for you to discuss your loved one's death and to use the word *suicide*.

- Second, when you openly and honestly deal with your loved one's suicide, you will begin to experience personal healing.

- Third, you will ultimately experience ministry opportunities to help others who grieve the death of a suicide.

Everyone who knew the deceased may feel the stigma of suicide, including the spouse, parents, siblings, extended family members, and close friends. We all feel the agony of suicide. A few within the circle will speak of the suicide openly and freely. Most just quietly acknowledge the circumstances of death, and a few will not even admit death by suicide.

Parents especially feel the pain of death by suicide, wondering what others must think of them. Parents mold children at the earliest ages and literally pour their lives into their children. They do their best to lead, guide, and train, but now the unthinkable has happened. They ask themselves, "Where did we go wrong?" The layers of guilt and shame can be overwhelming. Added to those unmanageable emotions, they may hear, or think they hear, their friends questioning their parenting choices.

A parent deals with all the "if only" of death. "If only we had not divorced"; "if only we had not argued"; "if only I had not let my son go to that concert"; and the list goes on and on.

A counselor once shared with me that a suicide is seldom based on only one issue. The individual contemplating suicide usually is experiencing several diverse issues. We cannot blame ourselves for what we cannot understand and probably could not have prevented.

Spouses feel a unique responsibility for suicide. A marriage implies a direct responsibility for intimate care for each other. A marriage partnership is defined as a deep and loving relationship wherein we support one another. But marriage partners need to realize that the basic causes of suicide, especially a mental illness, far exceed the faithful loving care of the partner. Even the most dedicated spouse cannot overcome what a therapist and counselor could not do in preventing the suicide of the loved one.

A counselor friend of mine shared these thoughts with me:

> *"Humans are complex in their thinking, and they seldom make any decision based on just one reason. One of the things you must acknowledge is that*

*you may never know all the reasons for your loved one's death. Your peace will come when you realize you do not have to have all the answers to cope. This journey of finding peace may take you many months to achieve but you can get to that point."*

CHAPTER 14

# My Awesome Dad
## Diana's Story

*M*y dad died by suicide. I was extremely close to him, and on his seventieth birthday I planned to call and wish him well. But somehow, I mis-dialed his number and something else drew my attention away from the call. I did try to call him the following day, after his birthday, but we did not connect.

That same day, after his birthday, my brother called to tell me of my dad's death. He lived with my brother in his own side apartment. Dad chose death by suicide. He suffered depression, anxieties, diabetes, and heart issues. I was Dad's only daughter, and we were remarkably close. I struggled dealing with his death by suicide as he was a Christian. My birth mom experienced mental health issues and their marriage did not survive the strain. Dad remarried and my stepmother had health issues, and six months before Dad's death she passed away. After her death, my dad felt he had nothing left to do. He had shared he did not want to grow old alone. The day after his seventieth birthday, he died by suicide.

I believe at the time of his death he was not taking care of himself physically nor thinking straight. He was filled with constant anxieties, and I can understand why he did not want to live life alone as he was. It was a terrible way to feel, and he chose to end his life of pain. I cannot blame my father for his death; he was not in a right frame of mind. So, it is difficult for me to say he was totally responsible. Medications seemed to have changed his sense of healthy well-being; he was heavily medicated, maybe too much too soon. He took a lot of medications, which did not allow him to deal with his real issues.

Dad was a believer. He was active in his faith but never told any of us as his children how to have a personal relationship with the Lord. Eventually we all came to know the Lord on our own. At one time in his life, Dad did rededicate himself to following the Lord, but he always felt guilty that he had spiritually let us down. He was not a frequent attender of church services. He mostly felt undeserving of God's love. At his memorial service, his death by suicide was not shared.

### Stigma of Suicide

One of the hardest issues I had to deal with was the immediate response of my stepfamily. They immediately took over all the arrangements. I am not sure why or how, but it was decided that his manner of death would be kept private and confidential. I felt we were keeping this information "under wraps." Dad was suffering from heart failure so that was an easy response when asked how he died. I am not sure even the pastor at the memorial service knew the real cause of his death. No one in the family wanted to talk about Dad's death by suicide. They reframed the truth concerning his death and decided to cover things up. I do not know if they all agreed before I arrived or if the first family that arrived made this decision.

When I arrived for the service, the family told me what they wanted me to do and share. This was not implied but expected of me. Many friends at Dad's memorial service asked me what happened, and I felt like I had to lie, to cover up his death by suicide. I could have become angry at my family, but I chose not to. They meant well. Anger and bitterness could have torn our family apart. We do love each other despite all that has transpired. We are not perfect–like all families God is working individually on each of us. Over the years I feel as though our family has become closer and loving.

## Guilt and Anger

In learning of Dad's death, my first immediate response was guilt that I had not reached him on his birthday. My second reaction was anger. I went from guilt to anger within a few minutes. As we progressed through the first several days after his death and service, we all still shared with others that the cause of death was due to heart failure. I knew I was lying, but I justified that maybe it was not truly a lie because he did have health issues. Still, I felt deceitful. I believed I had to honor the stepfamily's decision regarding cause of death because they wanted to keep it "under wraps."

Death by suicide is a traumatic event for survivors of suicide. We experience numerous questions that have no answer. My guilt focused on the fact that I grieved because I had not called my dad more often. I wished I had been more in touch with his feelings. So many things I felt I should have done. Sometimes we as grievers want to take on that responsibility. We convince ourselves "it really was my fault." The first thing I thought about and focused on was the guilt—how this was my responsibility, my fault. I wondered how I could have missed the signs. The harsh processing (accepting) through guilt added to my pain, heartache, sorrow, and grief. I felt as though I were in an emotional prison.

I felt so all alone in this process, but at the same time I could not come out of my own feelings. I felt like everyone else had taken over, telling me what I should think or feel about suicide. I felt like all my choices were deliberately removed and I had been left out of the process, and this increased my guilt. I felt guilty but I *was not guilty*. Guilt is telling you a lie and that lie is not from God. I found that my faith, trust, and hope in the Lord was my sustainer. It is not always our choice to grieve, but it is our choice how we grieve. Unhealthy grief is blaming yourself. Guilt wants us to keep ourselves in turmoil. God's love for us has not changed; neither has His plan for our lives.

*Forgiveness and Healing*

Growing up I understood the importance of forgiveness. I learned it through family and life experiences. We cannot hold on to anger; it creates an inward bitterness. We are to forgive as God has forgiven us (Colossians 3:15). I knew that was what God wanted me to do: forgive my dad. God had forgiven him, and I needed to also. That truth helped me a lot. Not in an instant, but willfully choosing to believe that with right actions I could put my feelings in a right perspective.

God also tells us that He is "the way, the truth, and the life" (John 14:6). God showed me the truth of forgiveness. He did not want me to bottle up how I felt. Through that process I experienced peace. That is what forgiveness does, not so much for the other person but for us; we have a newfound freedom. I found myself free not to be angry at my father, but rather to love him, miss him, and grieve his death. God made everything okay for me. I still feel deep sadness; that is part of normal grieving and is okay. I knew God did not hold my dad's death against me and that my feelings of guilt were not valid.

I learned the value of the truth that we as

suicide survivors are not responsible for the choice our loved one made. God is sovereign; He is in control. He was not surprised at Dad's choice of death by suicide. It was God's decision to let Dad enter His heavenly home and I remain here in this earthly home. God freed me to be myself, not guilty and not fearful.

*Encouragement to You*

Through the years my husband and I have been able to share with others in our heartache. Many years ago, our young son died in an accidental shooting. Through our healing process we were able to minister through a grief group to others in pain and sorrow. I share this with you so that you can understand my heart.

Some of the wisdom I am sharing comes from having walked where some of you now walk. God graciously led us through our pain. Yes, there are still those special anniversary dates when memories cause me to reflect on my pain once again. But God gently leads us through pain to new hope for the future.

You will have to learn to walk through this difficult process called grief. Be truthful in what you share with others. If you do not, you will feel guilt over "hiding things" and it will complicate your grief. I found that when I could not discuss Dad's death in honesty, especially within our family, my guilt and pain became difficult to deal with. It is important for you to find someone, perhaps a grief group, you can share your story and your pain with. I trusted and relied on my ladies' small group. They encouraged me and were my support team.

If you are experiencing the stigma attached to suicide, it is important to speak up and share the truth, especially to others who deny or cover up the truth. When we lie or conceal our true hurt, we create our own isolation. We begin to feel like a captive within our own feelings and thoughts, and that can create confusion. As I have previously mentioned, I felt I had placed myself in an emotional prison of guilt. You can choose to move forward, not with guilt or pain but with confidence in God. Choosing to believe God releases you from the prison you created because of what others have done.

You will have to realize, admit, and accept that your loved one's death by suicide was not and is not your responsibility. We do not have earthly control over life. You can beat yourself up, but peace comes from our heavenly Father. God is God. He is sovereign. He was not caught by surprise at the death of your loved one. But He does have a plan for those left behind. We are responsible for our own spiritual relationship with God. Others are responsible for theirs. We are not responsible for someone else's decisions concerning life. God gives to us a healthy grieving process not based on our feelings but His love. God's love and grace means we do not have to stay stuck in our grief and we do not have to remain there.

CHAPTER 15

# *Survivor's Guilt*

"Survivor's guilt" occurs when you grapple with the question of "Why?" and conclude that you, in some way, should have anticipated and even prevented the death. You begin to process your own unfounded guilt by your powerlessness to prevent the death, which in turn can become your own inner, personal conviction that you should have or could have prevented it. You must realize that you were not the only influencer of their emotional stress. For healing to occur, you must realize the truth that you had no control over your loved one's actions.

Guilt is one of the most intimidating emotions you can allow in your life and the greatest complication in your journey of healing. Guilt is a fabricated faultfinder. It relies on genuine memories but reframes pictures in your mind so that what you know to be truth is replaced with a different representation. Truth walks with us down the corridor of our mind and reminds us of the facts. Guilt walks down the corridor of our minds, takes down the truthful picture, and hangs a new one with a different frame and caption. The caption reads, "You are the guilty one." When you allow yourself to believe you are responsible for your loved one's death, you experience emotional confusion. *You are not responsible for your loved one's death.* Say it out loud as often as you need, write it down, place it on the mirrors in your home and on your laptop. You need to accept that you were not the decision maker.

Why do suicide grievers blame themselves? After having read many articles on this question, I can only theorize that each of us has a strong notion that we should be able to control or prevent tragedies. When we are unable to do so, we feel the weight of guilt that we were not able to prevent it.

The questions surrounding "why" actually seek answers to something we could not control and cannot comprehend. The simplest explanation is that we feel like we should have prevented the suicide and we did not, therefore "I am responsible." Added to that is the difficult truth that perhaps we had a confrontation with the person and said something we now wish we had not. Or did not say something we think we should have. Also, we could feel this guilt because we believe we should have taken some preemptive action. Ultimately, you must take off the burden of guilt and conclude that your loved one made the decision to die by suicide. It was their course of action, their decision, their choice. Not yours.

Guilt is critical and disapproving, while

responsibility recognizes the facts. If you can acknowledge that you are not responsible for your loved one's death, you are on the way to resolving your guilt. The reality is that your loved one, experiencing what therapists refer to as clinical depression, would strongly imply death was not a rational decision of their own choosing. Grasping this truth will help you to not blame your loved one or accept personal responsibility for their death. You accept the tragedy for what it was: a devastating series of illogical decisions.

Survivor's guilt asks the questions:

- *"Why did my loved one die? Should it have been me?"*

- *"It would have been so much better if I died and not them."*

- *"If only it had been me, my loved one would have coped better than me."*

- *"I know this is my fault. I should have prevented the suicide."*

- *"If I had intervened, this would not have happened; it is my responsibility."*

Many times, in life we must release the questions that only God knows the answers to. That may not be the answer you wanted, but ultimately peace comes through our faith and trust in God. All the "What if?" and "If only" scenarios will, like a barrage of pictures, replay over and over in your mind. With all these complications come the loneliness, helplessness, sadness, and unrelenting despair. Unfortunately, without professional counseling you might experience flashbacks, nightmares, and social withdrawal. Do you still wonder why I suggest professional Christian counseling?

Your grief will most likely be private, silent, and introspective as you consider whether you are responsible for the suicide. Do not allow yourself to erroneously take ownership of it. One widow related her journey through suicide survivor's grief as a self-evaluation of who she was. Immediately after the suicide she began the blame game against mental health experts, medications, her family, and then herself. Filled with anger and regret, she slowly realized she needed to forgive her loved one, those in her circle of family and friends that had been critical of her, and even herself. To her, this wide spectrum of forgiveness did not mean she was at fault; it simply meant she was willing to finally recognize the responsibility for the death was not hers or anyone else's, and she was ultimately able to move forward. Today she still experiences some occasional nightmares, but in her healthy journey of grief she has managed to reconcile her questions.

You may already be angry with yourself for missing the signs, and thinking to yourself:

- *"If only I could have done something."*

- *"Why didn't I listen?"*

- *"It must be my fault."*

- *"Why didn't God warn me?"*

- *"Why didn't I know?"*

- *"Why did she not choose life over death?"*

- *"If only I had prayed more often for him."*

- *"I thought she was only trying to get attention."*

- *"I never understood he was struggling."*

- *"If only I had answered that text."*

- *"I should have known what was on his mind."*

- *"If only I had been closer."*

- *"Why didn't I seek intervention?"*

One of our struggles with the "I wish I had" thoughts is the reality that if you knew then what you know now, then yes, you would have said, sensed, or done something differently. But you did not know that. The clinical term for this thinking is "hindsight bias." Most of us use the term "hindsight is 20/20." When we look back to try and discern hindsight, we assume we knew something or should have known something we did not know. In essence we believe we should have anticipated an event, therefore preventing it. The result of this type of thinking is guilt. The difficult issue with hindsight is that it is not reality. On occasion I am asked this question: "If I give you a hypothetical question, can you provide me with a hypothetical answer?" My response is that I never give hypothetical answers because they are not based on truth. No matter how hard we try to blame ourselves, hindsight is not truth and not reality. Hindsight is really thinking, "If only I knew," but you did not know.

Time and again you will replay what you think you should have recognized, known, and anticipated, until the death eventually becomes "my fault." If you accept this ownership of another's decision to end their life, you will forever be haunted by those memories.

A person's suicide is not based on just one issue but usually on multiple layers of issues. If you can recognize and accept that, then your action or inaction had little to do with the actual suicide. You must remember that your loved one's suicide was based on various irrational decisions.

One reaction a suicide griever experiences with their loved one's death is the painful question "Why my loved one and not me?" The implication being that their loved one did not "deserve to die" and somehow "I could have died in my loved one's place." The pain of loss causes the bereaved to try and rationalize that their death would not have caused such gut-wrenching agony, and therefore they could or should have died instead. The deep hurt of loss is so great the bereaved would rather be the deceased and not the living.

I do not recall where I heard this statement, but it is profound in truth: "I do not know how much my guilt weighed, but when I resolved it, a great weight was lifted." The suicide of a loved one can be a terrible shockwave. Whether you admit it or not, you might feel judged by others for the failure of your loved one to cope. You may question your own "public image." You will experience those insurmountable questions of why you did not "see it coming" or "what did I do wrong?" After the initial shock you will need to privately acknowledge that the death was not your responsibility or fault. Your loved one made the decision to complete suicide; you did not make it for them. Your loved one's suicide is not your fault.

# SEGMENT 3

# EMOTIONAL PAIN

CHAPTER 16

# *Dealing with Your Pain*

Sometimes just expressing your grief does not help resolve your hurt. Your words do not communicate your pain or the great depths of anguish you sense. One of the best tools I have seen for grievers is to journal their personal and most intimate thoughts, reflecting their inner emotions. I appreciate reading authentic thoughts from grievers as they lay their heartache before the throne of our Lord. On occasion I have read impactful devotionals from grievers on social media, and I am encouraged by how quiet times with God became crucial to their healing. Some people will plant a remembrance garden, write a book, develop a social ministry, and so many other options. But the key is to discern what works best for you. What will bring stability and peace back into your life?

Your journey of grief in dealing with loss of a loved one by suicide will be tumultuous, with twisting and turning roads. The path includes anger, heartache, questions, and legal issues all intersecting at the same time, so it is difficult to discern which

direction or road needs to be taken first. In fact, you
are traveling all these roads at the same time, with
every turn producing unsuspecting detours or speed
bumps. It is not unusual for suicide survivors to wish
they could go back to the time before their loved one's
death. But you cannot go back in time—the past is
closed. You begin to ask the question "What now?"
knowing the only true answers can be found in the
Lord. At the same time, you just want to be left alone
but you find yourself inundated with questions you and
others just cannot answer. Well-meaning friends' pry
into your personal life. The local deputies interview
you time and again. Families and friends request
information on the memorial service, but you have not
finalized any details with a funeral home. You want to
scream, "Leave me alone!"

At the very time you just want to bury your heart
in grief, you must deal with insurmountable details.
One wise suggestion I heard is for you to discern a
personal confidante, someone who can be trusted
to share your thoughts and needs with others, a
mediator to bridge the gap between you and the many
expectations now thrust upon you.

The survivor of suicide experiences incredible
roller-coaster emotions such as guilt, nightmares,
confusion, anger, and a sense of numbness. If you
were a witness to or present at the scene of the
suicide, these and other emotions are profound
throughout all your time of grieving. You need time

to process your emotions. It is critical that you not react to them but work through them. Your emotions are real. You cannot deny them but do not react to them. Acknowledge them but do not reject them or try to bury them. Accept them for what they are—your gut level wounds representing the death of your loved one. Allow yourself time to grieve and accept what you are feeling.

It is so important to share your feelings with someone whose confidence you trust. Your friend may not completely understand what you are experiencing but they can listen without judging your sometimes-unsubstantiated thoughts. Many times, just knowing someone listened helps balance your emotions.

# CHAPTER 17

# *Surviving Each Day*

*I*n the early weeks following suicide, many in bereavement will strive just to survive the next hour, the next day, and the next week. You have experienced unbearable emotions, feelings you never want to experience again. Tragedy places an insurmountable wall of disbelief and deeply embedded questions you probably cannot answer. I once heard "The moment I learned of his death I wanted to scream, but I couldn't. I wanted to understand what the police were telling me, but my mind would not function. I had always felt strong, but in a moment, I was on my knees weak and helpless. I tried to think calmly but all my nerves were quivering."

One day we are with our loved one, and without warning we are left with an indescribable loss. The plans with your loved one and family for tonight or tomorrow are now forever changed. The heavy pain upon your heart makes it almost impossible to speak or move. You may experience profound weariness and exhaustion. You find yourself just wanting to close your eyes, sleeping the next few months away. You cannot allow yourself to stay there. God has promised hope beyond today, comfort and compassion.

I once heard these thoughts from one who experienced loss by suicide:

> *"I feel as though I have no physical or emotional ability or desire to go on. I am completely drained, as though I have a debilitating illness. It almost seems as though this death has destroyed all purpose for my life. The depth of my hurt and pain leaves me profoundly powerless to grasp what has happened and unable to deal with life."*

The reality of loss by suicide is that it creates an immediate and terrible emptiness in the foundational structure of your life. Like every form of death, your emotional temperament has been forever changed. With suicide, however, this sense of loss may continue longer than other causes of death. While family and friends return to their daily routines, you will find that you and others closest to the deceased often struggle with powerful emotions. Several years after a widow's husband died, she shared the following:

- *"It seems impossible to leave home, yet I do not want to stay at home."*

- *"It would be wonderful to have someone visit, and yet I do not want any visitors."*

- *"How often I have wanted to share the details of his death, but I just can't."*

It was so difficult for her to convey her grief story. Some of her friends did not understand, some chose not to listen, and quite a few could not handle the sensitivity. Most felt uncomfortable, and eventually, except for few friends, she stopped trying to share about his death. Quite often it can be exceedingly difficult to share our pain. Not because we do not know how to  but that the grief pain is almost impossible to describe. Unfortunately, she found that while many friends did not want to listen, some wanted her to share too many details, including where and how they found the body and how he died. She quickly realized she had to discern with whom to share and how much to share. You will find yourself reliving the events of your tragic day repeatedly. We rehearse past trauma to make sense of it. When we relive trauma or share its story, we are trying to work through the details expecting some form of resolution. Someone once shared this thought with me "I want to share heartache's pain with my dearest friend, but my loved one's death is the cause of my pain." There is one friend who is always by your side, within your heart, and comforting you...the Lord Himself.

One of the challenging emotions of loss by

suicide is the sensitivity of feeling afraid, the reality of being alone, and a sense of impending danger. Your loved one's death by suicide may leave you with a profound fear of the unknown. In your mind you are trying to figure out the why of their suicide and your questions are a bottomless dark pit with no answers. You know the death is real, but you cannot comprehend any reasonable solutions or answers. A friend of mine was desperately trying to understand what happened. She shared the following:

> *"This morning I was pouring milk on my cereal, and I had just emptied the milk container. Looking at the empty carton, I thought to myself how much it reminded me of my emotions surrounding his death. The carton was empty, filled with nothing but a hollow space. Just like the empty carton, my life is now vacant. I could put the empty container back in the refrigerator, pretending it is full, but it remains void and useless. That is how I see my life, empty and useless."*

My friend ultimately did survive the traumatic death of her husband. It took time; she walked a lengthy journey knowing God would heal her hurt. During that difficult passage God sent special friends to minister to her. As she healed, she found herself reaching out and ministering to others. What was once a life without any hope, peace, or grace became a life filled with ministry to others in pain.

CHAPTER 18

# *Healthy Tears*

On your grief journey, you will experience incredible numbers of emotions. One form of grief I want to encourage you to accept is crying. Tears reflect your love, agony, and hurt. It is natural and healthy to cry. The difficulty is that your tears can cause others to feel uncomfortable. Most people will not know how to respond to your tears or know what to say. So, when confronted by your tears, people may share clichés like "Things will be okay"; "You shouldn't still be crying"; or "Your loved one would not want you to be crying."

Unfortunately, what happens when you receive this type of response is you stop crying in public. Even worse, you could convince yourself that your own tears are somehow wrong, and you will not allow yourself to cry. In one of my grief sessions, we had a widow who recently experienced the death of her husband. At the end of the second week, she told me she probably would not be back to the group because she would "cry all the time." Her tears embarrassed her, and she felt that others in the group would judge her. I reminded her, just as I remind you, that tears are a part of the normal grieving process, and it is perfectly okay to cry.

The Bible tells us that Jesus cried at the death of Lazarus (John 11:35). God knows the griever's tears. He understands your grief and sorrow, so why try to hide those emotions? Jesus shared for us the personal relevance of tears. A widow once shared with me, "I cried and cried until my tear ducts had no moisture left in them. I thought I was through with my tears, but my tear ducts filled up again, and I cried even more." Tears are valuable. They provide an overwhelming emotional release. Tears are perfectly healthy, soothing, and healing. So do not be embarrassed by your tears. You may even have to share with your friends that tears are a part of your healthy grieving process and say, "I am sorry if my tears make you feel uncomfortable."

Tears are our body's way of releasing wide ranges of inner emotions. We shed tears at joyful moments, such as the birth of a child, weddings, and in gratefulness. We also cry at difficult times, such as saying goodbye to good friends or watching our children leave home to start a new life. The most challenging tears are those shed as we experience the emotions in the death of our loved one. Tears of grief are a healthy sign of courage and strength, revealing our inner soul. These tears flow as a reflection of our great complexity of sorrow. Their release defines the authenticity of our heartache.

Grief is far greater than just the present time. I have listened to others who share that their tears lasted for years, unpredictably occurring when least expected. An individual shared it this way:

> *"My husband and I lived life as though writing a book, chapter by chapter. Some chapters were filled with fun, excitement, anticipations, or joyfulness. Other contained adventures in our lives such as travel and vacationing. Some chapters were stories of sorrow and heartache. Now the final chapter has been written. My book has been abruptly finished and closed. Maybe one day I will write a new chapter. I know one day I will move beyond where I am, I will heal. I know I will see my loved again in glory."*
>
> (1 Corinthians 15)

In my years of mentoring individually, and in grief groups, I have found that grievers who freely shed tears seem to heal sooner. When attenders of my grief groups apologize for crying, I immediately assure them it is good and healthy to allow the tears to come. When we try to hide or prevent the tears it only creates greater anxiety within us. I think God planned those tears to reflect love. Jesus showed that love in weeping for His friend Lazarus.

CHAPTER 19

# *Physical and Emotional Care*

*B*ereavement takes both an emotional and physical toll on us. As we work our way through grief, we tend to become so involved with emotional pain we neglect our physical needs. It is important for you to take care of yourself both physically and emotionally. We talk a lot about the emotional, but physically you must maintain a healthy balance through nutritious meals, exercise time, and proper rest. These may all seem difficult, but the result is a sound emotional balance, which is crucial to the grieving process.

It is critical in bereavement to maintain some form of daily routine. You have already noticed that the demands of your emotional pain have changed how you eat, sleep, and exercise. You must make a conscious effort to either establish or reset a daily plan for yourself. This might include some moderate exercise, small but nutritious meals, rest when needed, and certainly time for your emotional stability.

Perhaps when you first experienced disbelief of your loved one's death, the last thing on your mind was meal preparation. Sleep was not at all possible. I have been at memorial service meals where some well-meaning friend repeatedly tells a grieving family member, "You have to eat." It is interesting how our family and friends think that if you eat or sleep, you will somehow feel better.

I watched a movie last week where an individual's spouse had just died and her friend insisted she have lunch and a long afternoon nap, both of which she did. However, that is the movies; the reality is that it is not real life. In times of trauma, we tend to not want to eat, and sleep is at best elusive. This is particularly true of the initial days after experiencing the loss. However, after the shock of those first few days, it is vital to return to some form of healthy schedule. A lack of personal routine of individual care can eventually lead to emotional sadness.

I recall ministering to Barbara, whose husband had died, and she was convinced she was experiencing depression. I asked her a series of questions: "Do you go out and pick up your paper each day?" "Do you open your blinds in the morning, prepare your coffee each night, work through your bereavement, and pay your bills on time?" She answered in the affirmative to each question. Then I asked her a crucial question: "You used to go to your salon stylist every Friday. Do you still do that?" Again, she answered yes. I wanted Barbara to realize that she had developed a weekly routine of sorts, and that was helping her experience healthy grief.

Maintaining a healthy lifestyle will help you overcome your difficult circumstances and emerge from this tragedy an emotionally stronger person. You can overcome the intensity of sadness that you now experience. You can find happiness and meaning in life again. And you will be surprised at the times the Lord may use this journey of your life to reach out and minister to others.

I really appreciate the apostle Paul's thoughts in 2 Corinthians, that we as believers are a new creation, that old things have passed away and a new time has come (2 Corinthians 5:17). This scripture reminds us that as believers in Christ, we have been "transformed"; we are no longer who we used to be. Aren't Paul's thoughts relevant to your healing journey? You are no longer who you used to be because most every part of your life has changed. I realize Paul is stressing the importance of the new believer's life, but consider for a moment that in some ways, just like salvation, your life is now completely transformed. You are indeed a new person. You do not act or think as you used to. Your loved one's death has changed your lifestyle. You are a new creation, and just as you experience transformation into the life of Christ, grief changes your perspective of heartache in this life.

In Christ we have a hope beyond today. In

Christ we have a resolute peace. As believers we know that our Lord will work out all our questions and hurt, not only in this life but for all eternity to come.

CHAPTER 20

# *Learning to Breathe with Peace*
## *Nancy's Story*

My first husband died as the result of an auto accident. He was on his way home from work one afternoon when a drunk driver crossed the center line, killing him almost instantly. We had been married five years and had a beautiful two-year-old daughter. I cannot begin to describe the devastation, emptiness, anger, and profound loneliness I struggled with.

In addition to losing my husband, I was suddenly a single mom. Our daughter cried for her daddy. Seeing her pain only intensified my grief, and the anger I felt toward the drunk driver. I knew the only way I would get through the pain was with Jesus. I clung to His promise to never leave me, and to the peace only He can give. My hope in Christ was truly an anchor for my soul.

Eventually my heart healed, and God sent another Christian man into my life. We married and were blessed with another daughter. I was amazed at how God restored my heart and gave me another chance at love. Several years into our marriage, my husband developed some medical issues. He was on multiple medications and struggled with some depression. One day he did not come home and was not answering his cell phone. A few hours later a deputy came to my door. He told me that my husband of twenty-three years had driven to an isolated area and taken his own life. I was shocked and thought, *This cannot be happening.* He was fine that morning. He had kissed me goodbye and said, "I love you" as I left for work.

I began replaying everything in my mind, and wondered, *How did this happen? What did I miss? What could or should I have done? What if I had called him sooner?* Having walked the grief road once before with my first husband, I knew what was coming— the pain, the emptiness, the heartache, and the overwhelming grief, which was compounded because it was due to suicide. I was so angry at my husband for taking his life, for causing my children and me that awful pain. I even felt a sense of betrayal.

That first night I fervently prayed, begging God to help me. I told Him I could not do it again. And then, in the darkness of my bedroom, I felt Him telling me, "All you have to do is breathe in and breathe out." I did not have to figure out all the answers to my "why" questions.

That experience helped give me a sense of peace and of being "free." From then on, when I would feel the grief overwhelming me, I would tell myself to "breathe in and breathe out." Honestly, even if I had the answer as to why my husband chose to end his life, it would not have made my grief journey any easier, because no reason would have been good enough for me—suicide is never the answer. My journey of healing was not just one day at a time, one hour, or even one minute—it was one breath at a time!

### Grief Lessons Learned

I want to share a few things I learned along this journey. First and most important, God is with you always. Second, this pain is not forever. We are listed in obituaries as our loved one's "survivors," and that is what we must do—survive the battle they lost.

People will try to comfort you, but honestly, most have no idea what to say. They bring food, offer to take care of errands, or offer you money. They want to do something to help ease your pain, but they can only offer little temporary comfort. The only lasting peace you will find is in God. The Bible talks about a peace that passes all understanding—a supernatural "God peace." It is real and will give you rest from your pain.

Your heart will eventually heal, but let it take however long it needs, and as it is healing, pour God into it. Talk to Him, read the Bible, and just be still with Him.

Surround yourself with encouragers. You know who they are. Most important, forgive—forgive people for insensitive comments and prying questions... forgive yourself for not preventing the suicide. We want to think we could have done something, but the reality is we could not. And forgive your loved one. Forgiveness may not change your circumstances, but it will change your heart.

With God's prompting and help, I made the choice to forgive a stranger who made a horrible decision to drive drunk, and my loving husband who made the horrible decision to end his life. At first, I did not feel very forgiving, but I continued to declare forgiveness, and eventually my heart felt it. Choose to remember the good and allow the pain and trauma to fade. There is no set time limit, and it may take longer than you want it to, but just hold on to God and breathe. Trust Him to show you how to not just survive but truly live. He will guide you, and one day you will look back and see how He was taking care of you because He is God, and that is what He does. He loves us "profoundly."

CHAPTER 21

# *Unwelcome Comments*

*U*nwelcome or insensitive comments and observations are made by people who really do not know what to say. I once heard a well-meaning person say to the griever, "I hope suicide is not hereditary in your family." This type of statement is so difficult to deal with. A counseling friend of mine told me, "Sometimes well-meaning people may be angry about the suicide and are attempting to vent that anger. Also, they feel they have to say something. It is as though they think their words will somehow allow the griever to suddenly feel better."

As the griever, you look for answers that will help you deal with feelings of shock, anger, guilt, and confusion. Instead, well-meaning family and friends may come alongside with never-ending platitudes, such as "He is so much better off now"; "He had been plagued by his own personal demons"; and the almost incomprehensible statement, "What a stupid thing he did!" I recall one woman whose bipolar sister had completed suicide, and someone told her, "You must be at peace now. You can finally forget her and move on with your life."

Insensitive comments almost seem demeaning to the deceased. Condescending statements may imply the person is better off dead. These unfortunate opinions drown out the positive ones. I am confident you received many positive condolences and perhaps only one negative, but your mind dwells on that one negative. In our pain and hurt, we emotionally wrap ourselves in grief, almost as though enfolding our arms around ourselves. Then in that moment of despair, the obnoxious negative comment seems to attack our soul. That one negative remark reduces us to profound pain, almost as though we believe it to be truth. It overcomes all other emotions. I once read about a person who shared this experience and said:

> *"I just want to lift my hands and swat that stupid comment away, just like it was a fly. I knew it was not a valid truth of my loved one. I chose not to allow it anywhere in my grieving process. I knew if I did not immediately deal with that thought, it would become the emphasis of my grieving process, blocking my entry to the healing process."*

I know you cannot ignore insensitive statements; they are like a knife into your heart. But you do have to deal with them. You cannot let them take residence in your mind. They will override all the sensitive, encouraging words from others. This person wanted to "swat it away." That is good advice. You must purpose not to dwell on the negative words, not to allow negativity to control you. You also must give up the right to be angry with the one who shared it, because anger can also control you. You must accept it for what it was—an insensitive statement not meant to harm but rather simply oblivious of what to say.

CHAPTER 22

# *Dealing with Anger*

*T*his may surprise you, but anger is a normal part of grief. You should not pretend it does not exist, but eventually you do have to deal with it. No one enjoys being angry, but it does happen and can be a healthy venting and release of emotional issues. My counselor friend once shared with me the following thought on anger: *"Grievers should not look for circumstances that support, verify, or validate their anger. Ultimately it is the strength, confidence, goodness, and grace of God that brings anger and grief to a healthy conclusion."*

Initially you may have been angry with your loved one for a seemingly senseless decision to end their life. You will most likely experience anger because of their failure to find a better way to resolve their problems. Your insurmountable wall of frustration, questions, and emotions leaves you reeling with emotional pain, and you have discovered your loved one's life was a great deal more complicated than you can even begin to understand. Grief is the result of our love. If we did not love the person, we would not grieve. Anger can also be the result of your love—resentment that someone you invested your life in has abruptly and unbearably ended that relationship. Anger represents your deep love for the person who chose to do that, and your anger must be dealt with.

While it is okay to be angry, you also must try to understand what happened. Unfortunately, your loved one's final thoughts might have been "You are better off without me." This is one of the heartbreaks of suicide. Your loved one arrived at an excruciating conclusiveness, incorrectly determined, and now that decision rips at the fiber of your heart. We recognize that with all relationships there may have been those times we wish we had said or did something differently. But the truth is, you did care, and you did love. We must grasp that what our loved one considered rational was not rational. It can be hard to accept that your loved one emotionally did not perceive truth. But if you can, it will enable you to cope with some of your anger. In the final analysis you may need to be satisfied with only partial or even no answers.

Anger offers nothing to your healing process. In grief it is the result of how you perceive someone treated you. Your loved one left you with no explanation. The intimacy of your relationship has been shattered, and you have been left with bewilderment and frustration. These emotions contribute to your underlying hurt and pain. Your anger can become a serious hindrance to healing, so while it is a natural emotion in your grief, you must deal with it. You will learn to forgive; you must forgive, otherwise you will not heal. As a survivor of suicide, the love you still embrace will enable you to move forward through this journey.

Some people, during your sorrow and pain, may cause deeper pain by seeking personal information concerning your loved one. These are a group of people I like to call the "suicide detectives." Some will ask pointed questions, seeking all the details. I recall one griever sharing with me how after the death of their son, an individual asked so many questions they felt as though the police were questioning them again. Sometimes a well-meaning person will act like a detective, wanting to know all the details. This griever finally, with exasperation, told the inquirer, "Your questions are irritating. Please leave us alone." Remember, protecting your grieving heart is more important than answering insensitive questions.

I know that when a friend of mine died, I experienced a sense of loss, heartache, sorrow, and emptiness. The realization of his life ending far too young brought me unique regret about the loss of a friendship, a future never fulfilled, and the tragic loneliness of his wife and children. I found myself angry at the person who sold him the gun, the police department who after his first attempt was required by law to return his gun to him, and the mental health care workers who seemingly never found the right medications. I became angry because he never considered what the extreme consequences of his death would mean for his family. I do not think he realized, in the depths of his own illness, how his wife and children would wake every night with thoughts, memories, and the trauma of his suicide. The result of blaming someone else is that you will cultivate anger toward them. Initially this may seem reasonable but given time you must learn to forgive.

The apostle Paul, in Ephesians 4:26, exhorts us not to be angry. I know that each time I have ministered to the grieving after suicide, someone in the family or circle of friends expressed to me their anger at the one who died. Anger related to dying by suicide is the result of feeling betrayed, frustrated, powerless, and treated unfairly. Every time we dwell on our loved one's death, certain triggers of emotion spring up within us, causing our anger.

The key then is how we deal with anger. Not by validating it, sharing it, or lashing out unfairly but rather by allowing the grace of God to overrule it. Our anger can be focused in a God-honoring way. The apostle Paul, in sharing we should not let the sun go down on our anger, is not focused on an actual sunset. His point is we should not let time go by before dealing with anger. Otherwise, anger becomes bitterness, which in turn does not honor our Lord or our loved one. We do want to live with anger; we want to deal with anger.

CHAPTER 23

# *Betrayal and Rejection*

*O*ften when ministering to survivors of suicide, I hear how, because of their loved one's death, they feel rejected by the one who passed. You may have experienced your own thoughts of personal rejection. To think your loved one may have reasoned that you could live life without them is a devastating thought.

Death by suicide causes a layer of grief and a sense of betrayal that no other form of death leaves behind. The most devastating part of suicide is the lack of any final answers to all the questions. And you will never, with any finality, tie all the loose ends together. Bereaved individuals work their way through grief, but never forget their painful heartache. Right now, it may not seem as though you will ever be normal again, but you will learn through God's grace, close friends, loving family, and wise counseling to live life once again.

Betrayal is the feeling that your loved one left you without any regard to the horrible emotional distress it has caused you. You trusted and loved them. You built an entire life and future with or for them. You planned your life and world around them and expected them to be there for you. Then, seemingly of their choosing, they abruptly ended your loving relationship. No discussions, just an immediate ending. Most often in normal breaks of relationships, the person tries to share why and lets us know the relationship is ending. Suicide is not like that. It is sudden, with no understandable reason or discussion; it just ended. One loved one expressed it this way: "His suicide was just as deliberate and final as turning off a light bulb. It just suddenly gets dark." Another shared this thought: "She betrayed me. Just like that. No phone call, no message, no note, no warning. She just left, breaking off a loving relationship. How could she? I trusted her to be here today, tomorrow, forever. But she betrayed me by ending her life. She ended our relationship. How can this be?"

Betrayal is emotionally difficult to process with few answers. One way of dealing with betrayal came from a grieving individual who eventually found a way to move past the feeling that their loved one had thoughtlessly left them behind. Just like other emotions, the answer they found for betrayal was forgiveness:

*"I guess I must forgive because I will never understand. I do not want to be*

*angry and bitter or spend the rest of my life asking the "why" questions. The only reasonable answer I can understand is to forgive. Tough, but I must learn to forgive."*

This is the best answer I have heard, and it is truthful. You forgive your loved one. You will never know the why, and if you are to heal, you will have to choose to forgive the one who is gone.

CHAPTER 24

# Indescribable Loss
## Dawn's Story

*H*i, my name is Dawn and welcome to my story of God's grace and healing in my life. How can I even begin to describe the pain and loss of my dad and then my sister by suicide? Two loving and caring family members were suddenly separated from us. Coping with death by suicide is a unique journey. It leaves you asking questions for which you may have no answers. In sharing my journey with you, the heartache I endured and my walking through a deep valley, is an honest admission of my pain. It is also an encouragement to you that you will find your way, you will heal and while the scars remain, you will live life again. It is my desire to encourage you emotionally beyond where you might be at this time.

### My Dad

My dad was a complicated mixture of a person. He was a wonderful father, full of life. Dad was behind the planning of every holiday season in our family. He was the glue that held us all together. And yet, because of personal struggles, my father was also the one who brought great chaos to our family. My dad had such a huge heart for people who struggled in life, but many days he was sullen and withdrawn from his own family. Often our own family lacked the joy he provided so easily to others.

On the morning of Dad's sixty-seventh birthday, I decided to take him out for a birthday breakfast and, more important, so we could just talk. My dad told me just how proud he was of me. He knew I had come through some exceedingly difficult times in recent years–years filled with heartache, challenges, and trials. I was especially excited because my dad and I had been able to heal our relationship just prior to my family's move to Florida. Our relationship had been strained for many years and I had carried a lot of bitterness toward him. But through a gracious work of the Holy Spirit, I had been able to completely forgive him, and for the first time in almost forty years, we were building a new father-daughter bond.

When my father died, I had to process an awful lot of emotions. I felt like saying, "Wait a minute, God. I have gone through forgiveness, and Dad and I were in the process of restoration. What do you mean he is gone?" That was how I really felt. I vividly remember walking into Mom and Dad's house. Everybody was stunned–not just from the sudden nature of his death but because he chose death by suicide. I remember looking at my mom and breaking down in tears, crying, "I'm not ready for him to go." I felt my dad and

I still had a relationship to complete. It was as though I was losing the relationship I had always wanted with him. I remember experiencing some feelings of abandonment in the weeks and months that followed.

I am so thankful I was able to spend real time with my dad, and forgiveness and reconciliation. The grief process was a little easier but certainly not less painful. My anger and bitterness had been wiped away. To me, forgiveness is wiping old things away; everything is new and fresh. I am so thankful my dad and I were able to find both the time and peace of forgiveness.

## My Sister's Death by Suicide

Five years later I lost my youngest sister to death by suicide. My sister experienced a difficult life both physically and emotionally. She really struggled. On Friday night, as I was driving home from the hospital where I worked, my sister reached out to me. She seemed extremely depressed during our conversation. I could sense she felt very alone, discouraged, and unloved. I tried to encourage her throughout our conversation, but none of my words seemed to connect with her. Since she had plans for that weekend, I suggested we meet for coffee on Monday. She seemed to cheer up ever so slightly at that suggestion, and we both said we were looking forward to getting together.

As our conversation ended, she became even

quieter. In this moment of quietness, she said to me, "I don't hear God anymore." I reminded her that she did not need to "hear" God to know He was there, and that God said He would never leave us or forsake us. I shared with her that we may not "feel" God, yet we know His power and presence. I told her one last time that I loved her. She paused and asked, "Do you really?" I told her I loved her deeply; she would always be a part of our family. We said our good-byes, and I hung up, looking forward to our Monday coffee time that would never come.

## Stigma of Death by Suicide

My parents had been attending their church for several years. In the months after my father passed, I discovered people there were not comfortable talking about my dad. I am sure, at first, that it was difficult because our family and so many of Dad's friends were still in shock. Most did not know what to say, how to say it, or even what to do. I do not think people fully recognized, in the weeks and months that followed, that we were still mourning my father's death. We had been deeply traumatized and needed much compassion, love, and outreach.

I thought people might have been hesitant to talk about my father or acknowledge him in any way because of his death by suicide. I am sure many felt that because of the way my father had passed, it would be too upsetting to the family to speak about him.

Even within my family people seemed uncomfortable talking about what had happened. I think many people were concerned about upsetting us or traumatizing us further.

It was so much different when my mom died of natural causes. Many friends came by with meals, flowers, and condolences, and showed they really cared. I remember thinking that if my dad had died of a heart attack, people would have expressed their concern and love for us to a greater extent. The sad part is that when my dad died, few people chose to personally share their condolences. Many friends remembered their good times with Mom, but not so much with Dad. I saw big differences in people being able to show their caring. It was not that they did not remember good things about Dad; it was just uncomfortable for them to share.

As I said earlier, I did not seem to struggle so much with having to forgive my father or sister for what they had done, but I did struggle with shame. Because of the stigma that comes with death by suicide, I found I was sometimes embarrassed when someone asked how my father died. I think this came as the result of comments I have heard people say about those who have taken their own life: "What a coward!" "They were so selfish." "How could they hurt their family like that?"

It hurt me deeply to think that this was how people viewed my father and sister. I knew of the struggles they both had with mental health. In some

Christian circles I still find a lack of grace toward people who struggle with mental issues. Believers struggling with mental health are sometimes thought of as not having spiritual strength, and unfortunately their salvation might even be questioned. I have often reflected on the complete work of Christ and that both my dad and sister knew the Lord. The grace of God assures me that both Dad and my sister are with Him!

*Healing*

In my journey of grief, I found I did not need to process forgiveness as much as others might. Those issues had already been dealt with in my relationships with both my dad and sister. God was with me in these tragic deaths, walking beside me. At times it is still overwhelming. Of course, a memory will sometimes trigger my pain.

The most important thing I have found to do is keep my personal relationship with the Lord active daily. A second way I found release from pain was writing in a personal journal. It was my way of pouring my heart out to my Lord. Additionally, it is important for you to have a friend who will sit and listen to you, someone who has walked this painful walk and can minister to you. This special individual cannot be there to judge the person who died but to really want to minister to you. You can try and be on your own, but you really need a friend or a group within your church family coming alongside to encourage you. Their counsel will be impactful in your life.

I would like to share that only through knowing the Lord Jesus can there be any hope in such a dark situation as having a loved one die by suicide. Only the hope of salvation through Christ alone will ever bring us through these dark waters. When reaching out to someone who is going through such a difficult time, reach out with your love, kindness, and compassion. And most of all, encourage them in God's mercy and grace.

CHAPTER 25

# Abandonment and Fear

You may experience feelings that your loved one deliberately left without any warning. They abandoned you and left you to deal with an enormous emotional burden, not caring about how you would feel. Abandonment creates a huge void. Have you ever lost something you use every day, such as your car keys or phone, and you cannot find it? We look in all the logical places where we usually expect to see it, but it is not there.

In grief, when we lose a loved one, we experience those moments when we expect, for a second, to see them but then immediately are jolted back into the reality that they have died. The phone may ring, and without hesitation we expect our loved one to answer. Often, we think to ourselves, "Oh I have to tell Arthur this," but Arthur is deceased. We want to tell that person something, but they have left us. Our loved one who was so familiar is gone and no longer present. That sense of abandonment is a strange feeling, one extremely difficult to cope with.

In suicide your loved one left you. You were not a part of that decision. Your loved one left you all alone.

Abandonment is the unimaginable thought, "I have deliberately been left on my own." In relationships we rely on trust and expectation. We trust our loved ones to be there for us. Suicide breaks that confidence. Unlike anticipated deaths such as terminal illness, we had no chance to say goodbye. Death was unforeseen. You are left with a great hollowness. Your anger toward your loved one for abandoning you may last for months on end.

I remember one time listening to the adult son of a mother who decided life was not worth living and ended it with the use of medications. He shared his intense anger at his mother for abandoning their family, for the deceit she must have perpetuated during the months before her death, and for deliberately leaving her body where she knew he would find it. It was incomprehensible to him that his mother would even consider suicide, let alone actually complete the action.

As he processed his mother's suicide, he recalled the exact location where he found his mom, the exact time, the clothes she wore, and even the details of her makeup and hairstyle. In his nightmares he recognized the EMT and police responders and relived those same horrific scenes repeatedly. He was shattered by the enormity of the tragic events. At every turn in their once pristine home were the reminders of death. He could not turn off the pain, and he relived his mother's suicide over and over. He did seek professional counseling and ultimately understood that his mother did not intend to leave behind the shock of agony and hurt.

He shared with me, "Ultimately my mom was searching for a way out of unbearable struggles of life which I knew nothing about. She chose to abandon me." This young man lamented over his mom's death, and it was even more burdensome because his father had died several years previous. He was one of the first people to share impressions of abandonment with me in grief counseling. He related how he had lost his dad to cancer and the emotion of no longer having a father and how difficult the first Father's Day had been. Now his mom was deceased, and he had no parents. The vast difference was that his dad had no choice in death, but his mom did.

Many times, adult children who have lost both parents have the sense of being an orphan. What this young man experienced is being orphaned by his mother's choice. Ultimately, he chose Christian counseling and even with such harsh memories he has once again learned to trust others.

Often in grief we can feel we have been left all alone. Our sense of isolation and hollowness comes from the absence of a loved one in our lives. We may feel a great void and a sense of numbness or dullness. The author of the book of Hebrews reminds us that our Lord never leaves or forsakes us (Hebrews 13:5). His point is that when we are in the darkness of night, the quietness of the hour, experiencing absolute loneliness or fear, we can know our Lord has not forsaken or left us. The Lord will never abandon you in your anguish. He is here, present with you. He hears your pain and soothes your spirit. Allow your loving heavenly Father's grace, peace, and comfort to embrace you.

CHAPTER 26

# *Fear of the Present*

S ometimes as a suicide survivor you will find yourself confused with an emotion that unexpectedly creates anxiety. You are waiting for a loved one to connect with you, or they should have arrived home some time ago. Your mind begins to wonder where they are, why they have not called, and an effort at social media contact becomes frustrating. We begin to wonder if something traumatic has happened. When we cannot connect with them for a few hours, it seems like days. The longer we are unable to reach them, the greater our anxieties increase. We begin to call close friends, neighbors, or their landlord, anything to try and reach them. We worry that maybe they experienced an auto accident or a home invasion. The time on our iPhone and watch seem to stand still. Three hours have passed and we ponder if it is time to call the local law enforcement agency. Let me assure you this is not an unusual experience. Over the years many people have recounted similar experiences to me.

It is important not to let your feelings overrule rational judgment. The probability of you experiencing a second traumatic event so soon after your current experience is remote. I do not have any statistics to support my assumption but my thirty years in ministry have substantiated my thought. Feelings are often based on what we think or what we feel, not on facts or reality. We allow our sensitive emotions to continue to imagine or write a new story. For example, the traumatic loss of a loved one leaves multiple layers of unanswered questions. We are still expecting another chapter. Some might refer to it as "waiting for the other shoe to drop" or "bad things come in pairs." We almost anticipate additional pain to occur. There is the intense fear that if "It happened once it will happen again."

In fear we have the expectation that something bad is happening to another loved one. Once we allow that fear to set in, we begin the process of reframing our fears. Reframing in grief is "telling yourself a different negative story" about the same events, or expectations of future events. It is dwelling on negative feelings and focusing on worse case circumstances. Reframing is taking a difficult situation and expanding unfounded feelings to further increase your anxiety. It is a preoccupation with allowing yourself to believe what your fears are telling you. Have you ever experienced changing the frame on one of your favorite paintings or pictures? Some frames enhance the picture; other frames detract from its beauty. I was visiting with my daughter and in her kitchen, she had a cross stitch her mom had made over twenty years ago. She decided it needed a new frame, something to make the cross stitch more vibrant. The frame she chose literally enhanced the thread colors and essence of the cross stitch. It looked more beautiful than ever. That was positive reframing. She was amazed at the immediate enhancement the frame made.

When we reframe our negative feelings anticipating another tragedy, we choose to picture circumstances in a different context than they really are. In essence we take our cares, concerns, worries, anxieties, fears, and we remove one frame of pain and loss to a different frame of greater expectation of pain and loss.

Nancy Self, Associate Director of Grief Care Fellowship, whose story is included in this and other Grief Care series, shares her personal experiences of reframing while in grieving. When Nancy was a teenager, her sister died. She experienced a great deal of anxiety that she would die also. There were no rational truths to her fears, but she allowed her emotional pain to reframe it. Later, as young wife and mom her husband tragically died in an auto accident, so whenever her second husband was late arriving home, she again reframed a past pain and feared her second husband would also die in an auto accident. It is through knowing the Lord's overwhelming grace and peace that she shares her testimony.

A second illustration is my wife and I. Recently our adult son unexpectedly and tragically died from health complications. Our only other adult child, a daughter, lives about an hour from us. She is wonderful at keeping in contact with and checking in on us. One night my wife was chatting with her on social media when suddenly for no apparent reason she stopped messaging. For an hour there was no response. She did not answer her phone and we began to worry something bad had happened. Perhaps she had a serious health issue. After two hours the level of anxiety only heightened. Why was she not answering her phone? We decided to call her property manager and have her check on her. To say our daughter was mystified at our actions was obvious. The fear we experienced stemmed because of our son's death. We allowed our fears of one experience to reframe another. We learned a valuable lesson-trust the Lord and not our emotions.

In both Nancy's and my experience, we anticipated something that was not a reality; we let our imagination and feelings dictate the moment. All of us can allow our thoughts to run vividly ahead of reality. Throughout this book we have been reminded not to trust our feelings but to trust our Lord as our steadfast counselor and anchor. He alone provides our wisdom and insight. When you experience those dreadful reactive emotions and distress, reframe your fear in the assurance of God's love, comfort, grace, and peace.

# SEGMENT 4

# HOPE FOR YOUR TOMORROW

CHAPTER 27

# *Broken but Healing*

S ometimes it is healthier and more beneficial to ask, "What now?" rather than "Why?" You need to consider how you will live your life from this point forward. What positive objectives and goals can you put in place and how will you achieve them? How can you let others into your hurting world in a new and different way?

You may want to discover new traditions to honor the memory of your loved one rather than dwell on your sadness. Perhaps you need to honestly ask yourself how your loved one might have anticipated your life to be successful, and how they would want you to continue in this life. Given appropriate time, one of the most significant parts of your grief journey will be to come alongside others to share your experience, insights, and wisdom. You will eventually learn how to allow yourself to become vulnerable again.

If you are by nature a positive person who realizes that even with struggles life is still worth living, your journey will be healthy. If you are generally negative about life, your perspective will complicate your grief and you should seek professional counsel. Additionally, if you discovered the suicide, or have feelings of intense guilt, please seek professional counseling. The shock, disbelief, and emotional numbness of such an experience can leave you with deep heartbreaking pain and you will likely need assistance in walking through your emotions. I once heard someone share that grief's healing is a cluttered journey and has no timeline.

> *"Just when I thought I was making improvements grief struck again. Or when I think I had it under control I would fall apart one more time. I realized through God's grace, that I was not getting worse, I was not losing my emotional balance, I was simply experiencing grief. Grief is messy, we work our way through it. There is one thing I found out in my journey of grief and that is that I knew nothing about grief. The reality is that I will never stop hurting, crying or forget my loved one. I do keep moving forward, looking unto my Lord with the expectation of His grace and peace. I have found Him to be my one continual faithful companion. He knows my frailty,*

*heartache, and sorrow. He is my great comforter."*

In the final analysis of this journey of grief, the griever needs to gain a meaningful and personal understanding of death by suicide. It is essential that you learn to reconcile an outwardly tragic death with your own purposeful conclusion of grief. At some time, you will resolve both your loved one's death and your own need to continue in your journey of life. You may never have any concrete answers to the "Why?" questions, yet in your own acceptance of the death, you will rebuild your life.

During your healing, one of the dramatic changes is realizing you have become a different person than you were. The past several months has initiated changes in life you may never have considered. As you now begin the process of living a new life without your loved one, nothing can or will be the same. You are a changed individual. Your insights have changed. Once you did not hear others' pain, now you do. You stop and really listen. Your family and circle of friends have become more important. You have learned to accept change you never wanted to. Your memories have become more pronounced and treasured. You are a different person emotionally than you were a few months ago.

Take a few minutes and consider all your changes. It has been quite a difficult journey, hasn't it? But through God's grace, you have walked through this valley of desolation complete with all the hurts and pains. How often did you find yourself seeking God's wisdom, grace, peace, and comfort? He was always there, wasn't He? You will always carry the emotional scars upon your heart, but maybe that is good. They are evidence of great love and great loss but can also be evidence of great faith that developed through your pain.

Perhaps through your walk of grief you have found a new sense of God's peace and comfort. I hope you are recovering your joy and love of life. I trust that the tender lessons you learned will help you minister to others who now walk in your previous footsteps. Won't it be wonderful if you are now secure enough in whom you are to reach out and minister to hurting people? This is the new you, a changed person in and by the grace of God, knowing where you have been and anticipating where you are going.

I encourage you to recount how the Lord has ministered to you in so many special ways. How have you changed in the qualities of truthfulness, transparency, mercy, peace, compassion, tenderness, love, and sympathy? Grief, while difficult and emotionally draining, can also be an awesome journey from gut-wrenching pain to hope and looking forward to a new life, asking, "What now, God?"

The apostle Paul shares a powerful thought

about ministry to others out of our own painful experiences:

> *"Praise be to the God and Father of our Lord Jesus Christ, the Father of compassion and the God of all comfort, who comforts us in all our troubles, so that we can comfort those in any trouble with the comfort we ourselves receive from God."*
>
> (2 Corinthians 1:3-4)

CHAPTER 28

# *Living Life Again*

*D*o you recall the children's poem "Humpty Dumpty"? He fell off the wall and no one could put him back together again. He experienced a great tragedy, not of his own doing. But the real heartbreak is that no one could heal his hurt and pain. While there are varied interpretations of this poem, the reality is, he and his world were broken.

Is that how you feel during this time in your life? Broken? Do you feel unable to be repaired? Perhaps left alone in complete despair? Life is ruined and shattered? Humpty Dumpty had no happy ending to his story. But you are not Humpty Dumpty, and you are not alone.

The psalmist in Psalm 147:3, instructs us that our Lord heals the brokenhearted and He binds (covers or bandages) their wounds. Psalm 34:18, reminds us that "The Lord is close to the brokenhearted and saves those who are crushed in spirit." These scriptures are a marvelous reminder that when we lose what was precious to us, God will enable us to experience healing from intense, emotional damage. God will heal the tragic wound you have experienced.

In a real genuineness, your heart has been broken. Your loved one's death by suicide may have left you staggering with inexpressible emotions. Added to your loss are the feelings of disillusionment with your loved one along with the questions on your mind of what your others may think. Many friends care about what you are going through; they care about your pain. The psalmist wants you to cling to the truth that God cares about your pain and loss. God hurts with your hurt and weeps with your weeping, and He knows your deepest heartache. God desires to heal your shattered heart. He is the one who is closest to your broken heart, because He is resident within your heart, and He wants you to trust Him. He alone is the one who will place the broken pieces of your life back together again. He will remove your anxiety, fears, loneliness, and when needed, your guilt that you are somehow responsible. Your loving heavenly Father will replace painful hurts with peace. No one else can provide His deep and abiding love. The memory of your loved one will be forever etched in your memory. You will make it through your pain; you will heal, and you will live life again.

Many years ago, I suffered a severe cut to my hand. It was deep, bleeding and hurt intensely. But it did heal. Today I have a large recognizable scar from that ordeal. Likewise, you have experienced deep hurt, and like a wound to your spirit, deep emotional pain. God will heal your hurt, yet you will always carry a "remembrance scar." You will never forget your loved one; you will never forget their suicide. God will heal your wounds and your emotions. Allow Him to soothe your agony and bring you peace.

Humpty Dumpty had no one to put him "back together again." God alone can put the pieces of your life back together again. Trust in His healing grace. Ultimately you must leave all your unanswered questions with God. Only He knows the emotions that were in the heart of your loved one. Our faith along with His grace enables us to trust when we do not see, know, or comprehend.

The harsh reality of suicide is that seldom are the causes, reasons, and actions discovered or understood. In my years of ministry, the one area of death that has perhaps left me bewildered and asking questions more than any other is death by suicide. It is important that you put your emotional and physical energy into your healing process. Having been with families in times of suicide, I realize this is a difficult suggestion, at least in the initial stage of shock and dismay. But if you sincerely desire to begin your healing process, it is necessary to actively engage in your own healing. There will come a time when you set aside your unresolved questions and begin to heal, as difficult as that will be.

I am not suggesting I understand the mental progression your loved one processed through. How does one become so emotionally distraught with life that ending it seems the only rational thing to do? How did your loved one validate that life was not worth living? What I have learned over the years is that suicide is an attempt to end suffering, both physical and psychological. Individuals with a mental illness do not think rationally; they seem to not connect to reality, perhaps not considering the consequences. They just desire release from their pain.

Another vital truth for you to recognize and accept is that your loved one did not die by suicide to spite you. That is, they did not intend to make their death inflict deep suffering upon you.

Please hear this urgent reminder: if you are unable to cope with the pain of your loved one's death, seek professional Christian therapy and counseling. Suicide is unique; each griever's journey will be unique. It is not unusual for grievers dealing with loss by suicide to seek professional counseling, and that is healthy. This book is written to assist you through a difficult process of grief, but your pain and loss may be greater than you can deal with. Do not see professional care as a sign of weakness. It is not weakness but strength of your character to admit that you need professional counseling.

As you consider moving forward, it is imperative that you have dealt realistically with your grieving process. If you are to minister to others in the future, you must be able to share your experiences while not minimizing the pain of the ones you minister to. I have been blessed to have many folks over the years become grief group leaders. The one important observation I have made is that if the group leader is still currently dealing with a lot of pain, anger, and frustrations, that leader will bring those current reactions into the group.

While not completely healed, can you answer the following thoughts in the affirmative? Or are there still issues you need to work through?

- *"I have hope beyond today, a spiritual promise of healing."*

- *"I have accepted I am not responsible for the suicide."*

- *"I realize the death by suicide was not because of me."*

- *"I realize there was nothing I could have done to prevent the suicide."*

- *"I have realized suicide was my loved one's decision."*

- *"I understand my loved one was not acting rationally."*

- *"I have forgiven myself for not saying or doing something different."*

- *"I realize there are no easy answers to "Why?" but I am at peace."*

- *"I know and understand questions that I did not at the time of the suicide."*

- *"I have learned to not answer hypothetical or hurtful questions."*

- *"I have left my unanswered questions with the Lord."*

- *"I have forgiven my loved one and am no longer angry, bitter, or resentful."*

- *"I am now looking forward to the future— I choose not to live in yesterday."*

- *"By God's grace I will share with those who walk where I once walked."*

You will need to keep the loving presence of family members and friends close by your side. They can be mentors and companions who come alongside without judgment or endless questions, comforting you in your times of pain and sorrow. Their expressions of love and care will allow you to heal at your own pace and not at the expectation of others. Sincere friends allow you to spend time in your own private thoughts and yet will encourage you as needed. Recovery from a suicide of someone close to you is an immense task because the process of mending your broken heart is agonizing and slow. Your road to recovery requires that you depend upon not only family and friends but especially on your faith.

Seek to experience both physical and emotional healing. What does that look like? I do not know if you have ever done any mountain climbing. My experience is quite limited. I remember a time climbing a mountain with others and our lead guide told us it would be a three-hour climb. Less than two hours passed, and thinking we were near the peak, we thought we were making excellent progress. Our guide told us no, and in fact we were way behind his schedule. What we learned was that as you climb higher mountains, you come upon small plateau areas that may look like the peak. But as you observe your surroundings more intently, you realize this is not the peak, only an area that previously blocked your view of the true distance yet to go. We could not stay where we were; we had to continue our journey, as difficult as it was.

That is how your healing journey will seem sometimes. You will think you have experienced all you can experience and that the journey is over, and then you realize you still have further to climb. My point is you must focus on your walk with the Lord. He is where you need to focus for your goal of healing. You must keep your eyes focused not on the here and now but on where your Lord desires for you to be.

You are not just a survivor of suicide or just a victim living within the pain of suicide; you are a child of God. Our heavenly Father desires that you see beyond these difficult times of your life. His character of love, grace, and comfort embraces you. You will heal and you will live life again. God will guide you, but you need to take on that responsibility. No, you will never forget this gut-wrenching, tragic event, but you will find peace during heartache.

At the center of your hope is God's promise of His purpose and significance for your life. You have or are in the process of giving your hurt to God. Only God has given you this desire to live again; He alone has been your comfort, guide, encourager, comforter, and giver of insight. The continual hope of tomorrow, promised through His Word, has given you the purpose to daily move forward through your pain into His promises of new life. Your future, planned by God for you, is now yours to begin to live. It is ultimately your personal choice to accept His great promise of plans for your future. How do you now envision your new future? Are you ready to start living life again?

Here are some important considerations as you continue your journey of healing, moving forward and living life again:

- Former expectations of life have changed; you have new anticipations.

- You will still experience unexpected "triggers" on special days.

- You may continue to experience "triggers" of pain when least expected.

- Purpose to stay connected to those who have ministered to you.

- Accept that it is okay to laugh and enjoy life.

- You can and will live life again. By God's grace you will heal.

CHAPTER 29

# *My Friend's Suicide*
## *Francis Welch*

*I* would like to share with you my personal testimony of my grief journey when a close friend died of suicide. As Pastor of Care, I minister to the grieving and visit people in hospitals, nursing homes, assisted living facilities, rehabilitation facilities, and in their homes. My friend, as his schedule would allow him, loved to travel, and visit with me. He was incredibly upbeat. He outwardly loved life and people. His intense use of funny stories and antidotes, along with his loud boisterous laugh, could cheer anyone's day. There was almost nothing he would not do for someone if it were within his ability to do so. He met a person's needs with a boundless sense of urgency and enthusiasm. Yet in the privacy of his own emotional world, he experienced the consistent bombarding of personal disparaging thoughts. Those deep, dark emotions were not unknown to his family or me.

Over many years he attempted dying by suicide in various ways, never succeeding, or perhaps never desiring to succeed. I learned from these experiences that the "authorities" asked him if he had bullets with him or just the gun, and his wife experienced the anguish of various physical injuries he inflicted upon himself. Then one evening he again told his family he was going to kill himself, went out by the poolside, and died by suicide. He was immediately transported to a hospital trauma center. The gunshot wound, however, was fatal, and throughout a long traumatic night, his wife and family began the "notification" to family and friends. We spent time talking with and listening to medical authorities. The phone rang almost incessantly, and with morning came the necessity to plan his memorial service.

That evening and in the following weeks, as both friend and pastor, I dealt with layers and layers of emotional issues and the endless questions of "Why?" Yes, my friend certainly had emotional issues, yet the question still lingers today: "Why?" For me, it was exceedingly difficult to minister with the family in their journey of grief while also trying to experience my own grief in the loss of my friend.

I spent time with them, and for my own journey of grief I visited the small community park a short distance from their home. It was a park where my friend and I often sat and shared thoughts of the Lord. I also recall he liked one of the most "off the wall" restaurants where they served a red cabbage soup. It was unpleasant to me, but he loved it. Even today, many years later, that little shell of a building stands, and although long since out of business, it remains a reminder of the loss of one of my good friends.

I share my personal experience with you so you may understand that as a griever, you will also be allowed to share your journey with others as an encouragement to them. It will not be easy, your recovery will not be quick, but your personal experiences will enable you to become an encourager. So, learn from your experiences and learn wisely.

I have an absolute assurance of meeting my friend in heaven. He loved the Lord. I, for one, can never explain all the emotions he experienced. But one thing I am certain of is that the Lord has promised us in Romans 8:38-39 that we shall never be separated from Him, whether in life or death. As a griever, your life is forever transformed. You will always miss your loved one, but you will survive. And like my widow friend, you will once again experience a healthy, content, meaningful, and influential life.

CHAPTER 30

# *Closing Thoughts*

Whe have shared time dealing with the emotional pain of grief. Likely you have experienced many of the hurts and emotions we have explored. I also know you have experienced many more we have not shared. However, those we have covered are some of the major challenges survivors of suicide encounter. In your grief journey, you need to recognize and learn to work through these difficult and deep feelings. You cannot bury your upsetting and demanding emotions. You cannot go around, over, or under them; you must work your way through them. Your healthiest way, as a survivor of suicide, is to trust your Lord to lead and guide your journey. A familiar maxim says, "Time heals all things," but this is only partially true. I would add, "What you do with your time heals."

The trauma created through death by suicide can be overwhelming. You will have to work through your pain, but as you allow the Lord to guide you, you will experience healing. Some of the emotional scars will last your lifetime but working through your grief will help you recall and cling to loving and treasured memories.

Working through your grief does not mean you forget your loved one. That will never happen. But it does mean you learn to live life again with peace. We trust the testimonies shared by individuals who have walked where you now walk will be of great encouragement.

Blessings, grace, and peace

Francis Welch

CHAPTER 31

# *Encouragement from the Scriptures*

*"The LORD himself goes before you and
will be with you; he will never leave you
nor forsake you. Do not be afraid;
do not be discouraged."*
(Deuteronomy 31:8)

*The LORD is my rock, my fortress
and my deliverer;
my God is my rock, in which
I take refuge,
my shield and the horn of my salvation,
my stronghold.*
(Psalm 18:2)

*The LORD is close to the brokenhearted and
saves those who are crushed in spirit.*
(Psalm 34:18)

*My flesh and my heart may fail,
but God is the strength of my heart
and my portion forever.*
(Psalm 73:26)

*My soul is weary with sorrow;*
*strengthen me according to your word.*
(Psalm 119:28)

*I lift up my eyes to the mountains—*
*where does my help come from?*
*My help comes from the LORD,*
*the Maker of heaven and earth.*
(Psalm 121:1-2)

*He heals the brokenhearted*
*and binds up their wounds.*
(Psalm 147:3)

*But those who hope in the LORD*
*will renew their strength.*
*They will soar on wings like eagles;*
*they will run and not grow weary;*
*they will walk and not be faint.*
(Isaiah 40:31)

*"So do not fear, for I am with you;*
*do not be dismayed, for I am your God.*
*I will strengthen you and help you;*
*I will uphold you with my righteous*
*right hand."*
(Isaiah 41:10)

*"Peace I leave with you; my peace I give
you. I do not give to you as the world
gives. Do not let your hearts be troubled
and do not be afraid."*

(John 14:27)

*So will it be with the resurrection of the dead.
The body that is sown is perishable, it is
raised imperishable; it is sown in dishonor,
it is raised in glory; it is sown in weakness,
it is raised in power; it is sown a natural body,
it is raised a spiritual body. If there is a natural
body, there is also a spiritual body.*

(1 Corinthians 15:42-44)

*Praise be to the God and Father of
our Lord Jesus Christ, the Father of
compassion and the God of all comfort,
who comforts us in all our troubles.*

(2 Corinthians 1:3-4)

*For we know that if the earthly tent we
live in is destroyed, we have a building
from God, an eternal house in heaven,
not built by human hands.*

(2 Corinthians 5:1)

*For I am convinced that neither death nor life, neither angels nor demons, neither the present nor the future, nor any powers, neither height nor depth, nor anything else in all creation, will be able to separate us from the love of God that is in Christ Jesus our Lord.*

(Romans 8:38-39)

*But our citizenship is in heaven. And we eagerly await a Savior from there, the Lord Jesus Christ, who, by the power that enables him to bring everything under his control, will transform our lowly bodies so that they will be like his glorious body.*

(Philippians 3:20-21)

*Praise is to the God and Father of our Lord Jesus Christ! In his great mercy he has given us new birth into a living hope through the resurrection of Jesus Christ from the dead, and into an inheritance that can never perish, spoil or fade. This inheritance is kept in heaven for you, who through faith are shielded by God's power until the coming of the salvation that is ready to be revealed in the last time.*

(1 Peter 1:3-5)

*"He will wipe every tear from their eyes.
There will be no more death or mourning
or crying or pain, for the old order of things has
passed away."*

(Revelation 21:4)